The Workshop Book

FROM INDIVIDUAL CREATIVITY TO GROUP ACTION

R. BRIAN STANFIELD
for The Canadian Institute of Cultural Affairs

 NEW SOCIETY PUBLISHERS

In memory of all those in ICA who worked with and developed this method over the last fifty years.

What is the knocking at the door in the night?
...It is the three strange angels.
Admit them, admit them.

D.H. LAWRENCE

Cataloguing in Publication Data:

A catalog record for this publication is available from the National Library of Canada.

Editors: Ronnie Seagren and Brian Griffith
Design and layout: Ilona Staples

Printed in Canada on acid-free, partially recycled (20 percent post-consumer) paper using soy-based inks by Transcontinental/Best Book Manufacturers.

New Society Publishers acknowledges the financial support of the Government of Canada through the Book Publishing Industry Development Program (BPIDP) for our publishing activities, and the assistance of the Province of British Columbia through the British Columbia Arts Council.)

Paperback ISBN: 0-86571-470-3

Inquiries regarding requests to reprint all or part of *The Workshop Book: From Individual Creativity to Group Action* should be addressed to New Society Publishers at the address below.

To order directly from the publishers, please add $4.00 shipping to the price of the first copy, and $1.00 for each additional copy (plus GST in Canada). Send check or money order to:

New Society Publishers
P.O. Box 189, Gabriola Island, BC V0R 1X0, Canada

New Society Publishers aims to publish books for fundamental social change through nonviolent action. We focus especially on sustainable living, progressive leadership, and educational and parenting resources. Our full list of books can be browsed on the worldwide web at: http://www.newsociety.com

Copublished by

NEW SOCIETY PUBLISHERS
Gabriola Island BC, Canada

The Canadian Institute of Cultural Affairs (ICA Canada)
579 Kingston Road, Toronto, ON Canada M4E 1R3

The Workshop Book

CONTENTS

PART 1. THE CONSENSUS WORKSHOP METHOD

PART 2. THE FINER POINTS OF THE CONSENSUS WORKSHOP

PART 3. WORKSHOP LEADERSHIP

PART 4. CONSENSUS WORKSHOP APPLICATIONS

ACKNOWLEDGEMENTS

Every achievement always stands on the shoulders of others. As mentioned in Chapter 2, this book derives from many sources. Here, I want to acknowledge the intellectual capital of ICA and its associates round the world who, for over four decades, have continued to develop and write about this method. In particular, I want to mention the stellar and pioneering work of Laura Spencer in writing *Winning Through Participation* in 1989. Her wisdom is quoted often throughout this book. I am also indebted to Terry Bergdall's application of the method in East Africa, documented in *Methods for Active Participation*. Jon Jenkins' *International Facilitator's Companion* has also been a great help. All those who have developed highly detailed manuals for training thousands of people from all walks of life in the workshop method have done a great service to society and to the development of this work.

Secondly, this book could not have been written without the regular input and coaching from ICA Associates staff in Toronto, who met Monday mornings to work with the author. I am referring to Duncan Holmes, Wayne and Jo Nelson, Bill Staples and John Miller — master facilitators have used the workshop method to move communities and organizations into the future from Kenora to Inuvik and from Vancouver to Miramichi. What came out of their mouths onto the pages of this book was freshly minted wisdom. The reader will learn things about the workshop method that have never, till now, been put on paper. Thank you, John, Bill, Jo and Wayne, and Duncan.

Particular thanks to Duncan Holmes, Jo Nelson and Daphne Field for their work on the manuscript, and to Wayne Nelson for being so willing to answer my many questions.

Duncan went over the method sections in fine detail, helping me rewrite many parts for maximum clairity. Jo rewrote the final chapters so they are much more helpful. Bill Staples was instrumental in supplying the digital photography which illustrates the book's ideas in so many places. Thank you, Bill.

Editors, Ronnie Seagren and Brian Griffith, as usual have done a superb job of keeping the author on the straight and narrow with their usual creativity and fastidiousness. Thank you.

I am also grateful to my colleagues and New Society Publishers for being deadline-merciful.

Over the last seven years, *Edges* has regularly published articles on facilitation and workshopping with examples from the field. Many of the rich paragraphs and examples from these articles appear in the book. Thank you, *Edges*, and thank you, *Edges* authors.

Finally, I am grateful to my wife for reading the manuscript and for her constant encouragement, and, especially, for her understanding when I arose at all hours of the night to work on *The Workshop Book*.

FOREWORD

Those who are familiar with ICA methods may wonder why ICA Canada would produce a book on the consensus workshop method at this time. The ToP™ consensus workshop method is at first sight very simple. Why have a whole book on it?

Like many elegantly simple tools, there is a wealth of profound thought and experience that underlies this method. Although merely following the steps at a surface level can get amazing results, many people wish to know why the method works so well, and how to get the most out of it. Knowledge and understanding of each part of the method, the whole process, and the propensities of human nature upon which they are built allow depth and sophistication in the use of the method.

This book intends to be a handbook that provides clear, practical, detailed procedures for applying the method appropriately. It is also a guide for adapting the method to large groups or small, for creating "quick and dirty" solutions or facilitating serious and deep dialogue toward a consensus. It also provides ways to vary the experience of the process when necessary for repeated use.

The book also intends to be a reference book for design and troubleshooting, as well as a ready source of "best practice" experiences. This can flesh out the learning from a training experience and clarify confusions.

Examples of focus questions that work, finished workshop products, and the process of synthesis provide templates for the facilitator to understand and design workshops that succeed.

We wish you success as you use this method with groups to harvest and refine their wisdom.

Jo Nelson
President, International Association of Facilitators

INTRODUCTION

A more collective process where all voices are heard and a diversity of
experience brought to bear on a problem produces a much richer form of
democracy than the top-down version favored by modern government.
Judy Rebick, *Imagine Democracy*

THE DEMAND FOR FULL PARTICIPATION

For whatever historical reasons, perhaps the sheer overwhelming size of organizations
and groups, there is emerging a strong demand from ordinary people to have input into
the decisions that affect their lives, and to have a chance to add their creativity and
insight to solutions. Wherever groups of people gather today to figure things out, make
decisions or solve problems, there is the question of who gets to participate, whose
wisdom will be heard, and what process will be used. We are familiar with public
meetings where a few people sit at the front on stage and tell the assembled people in
their serried rows what to think. Afterwards, the public may ask questions, but not offer
their own ideas. The process is top-down and condescending.

This is an example of a debilitating dualism that assumes that some folk are "right."
They are the ones with the answers. The rest of the folk are wrong or ignorant, with
nothing worth sharing. This is not to deny the role of experts in dealing with many
issues, but all too often those in power listen only to the experts, and not to the public at
large.

Changing the structure of such meetings and forums could give more voice to the public than simply inviting them to ask questions. I remember going to a public forum on "the water problem." The experts up on stage spoke, then people stepped up to the microphone individually to ask their questions. I thought, "What a difference it would make if, first of all, we were sitting around tables in full sight of each other. Then a facilitator could come out front with his clipboard, and pose a focus question to the full audience, experts included, such as: 'What can we do to deal with the water problem?'" People would be invited to jot down notes on how they would answer the question. Then the facilitator would write their answers onto the flip chart and help the group pull together their wisdom. Someone working in the background with computer and printer would have a document ready and printed up by the end of the session, so that everyone could leave with a copy of their work and decisions to work with.

The difference between the two processes is night and day. People's creativity is unleashed. They become a community dealing with a common problem. All participants have the opportunity to get their voices out. The experts have their turn, and the public has its turn. At the end there is a product to take home.

Greater participation, however, is tricky. Many of us have terrible experiences of meetings where the process encourages "participants" to speak. But here, one is lucky to escape with one's life. The attack dogs are loose. People are freely ridiculed while still speaking. Argumentation and often abuse fill the air. One hesitates to open one's mouth in this environment. Even parliaments are not beyond this. Anyone who listens to Question Time in the Canadian Parliament is aware of how easily the ideas of others are ridiculed and the speakers abused. Debra Tannen's *The Culture of Argument* describes a tendency which seems embedded in every part of society, appearing as soon as people begin to talk. This might explain the recent outpouring of books on dialogue, which are attempting to shift this culture and provide another viewpoint. It is possible, the authors say, for a group to converse and listen to each other with respect.

In the arena of business, strides are being taken to structure participation and mutual respect into decision-making. However in most hierarchically-organized companies, you keep your head low, do your job, and offer no opinions at all. The wellsprings of creativity are stopped up. Management finds little or no feedback from subordinates.

Many executives and workers assume that hierarchy obedience is the final form of the organization. But there are organizations today whose vision goes far beyond greater size or profitability towards higher maturity and fulfilment. ICA Canada developed the model below to describe emerging forms of leadership, participation, and organization. It shows four major phases in the development journey of organizations, of which the hierarchical organization is the most basic. (Figure A)

As the organization passes through the phases of the journey, the participation, interaction and collaboration of everyone involved reaches a higher level.

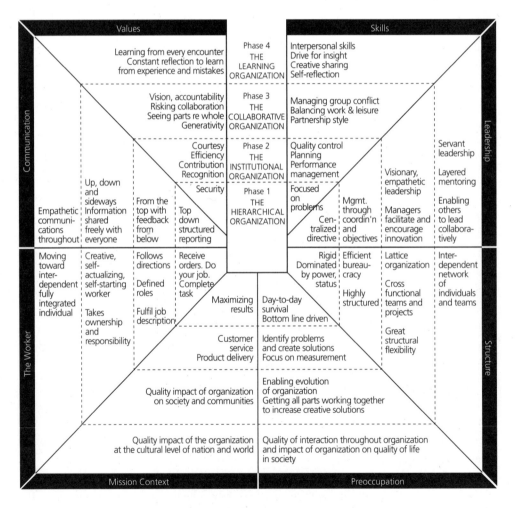

Figure A Map of Organizations

But with all this change going on, if we look in on the average NGO board meeting or association meeting, what do we still find? *Robert's Rules of Order* holding sway.

ROBERT'S RULES OR OPEN-ENDED QUESTIONS?

Enter *Robert's Rules of Order*. We owe a great debt of gratitude to their author, Henry Robert. First published in 1876, *Robert's Rules* gave enlightenment and comfort to frustrated members of associations who were easily victimized by overbearing chairmen and ruthless small cliques. The *Rules* armed members of societies and organizations with the know-how to combat those seeking to push through controversial resolutions without proper consideration. Historically, the *Rules* meant progress. For want of nothing better, *Robert's Rules* still serve a useful purpose.

While, historically speaking, the advantages of *Robert's Rules of Order* were many and obvious, so were the disadvantages. That book of rules now stands like a Colossus, barring the way to the real and all-around participation of large numbers of people. What blocks the way is the foundational image undergirding the *Rules* that the way you handle mass participation is by handing everything over to committees appointed by the chair. This way is considered less messy. The committee comes up with a model and brings it back to a large body, who either says yes or no to it. That is often called participation. Or the committee presents a motion, there is time for discussion, then they vote.

Participation here is taken to be the reaction to the discussion. In fact, the individual must be restrained somewhat if order is to prevail. The voting process is based on win-lose. There is no recourse for the losers of the vote. There are no opportunities for people to volunteer for tasks. You must be elected to a committee. And the committee does not come up with an action plan, but simply a report, which is "received" and voted on. The process can be so boring it can leave participants brain-dead. However, parliaments and organizations and boards still operate based on the *Rules* 125 years after their publication — either a remarkable testimony to their usefulness, or a witness to humankind's lack of imagination.

LEVELS OF INVOLVEMENT

Full-barrelled participation does not happen all at once. When it comes to decision-making, there is always a spectrum of levels of involvement.

Levels of Involvement in Decision Making

Responsibility for Planning and Action Implementing	Full Responsibility	8	Participants have full responsibility for all aspects of the given situation, project or organization.
	Decision-making Authority	7	Participants are authorized to make specific decisions within clearly defined terms of reference.
	Implementation Responsibility	6	Participants are designated to implement a specific decision or project.
Providing Input	Input toward Decisions	5	Participants provide ideas to be considered by those making specific decisions. Plans may be presented to solicit responses or open-ended questions may be asked.
	Input toward Implementation	4	Participants provide ideas on how a decision can be implemented.
Receiving Information and Services	Education	3	Participants are assisted in understanding decisions, how they are affected, and what is expected of them.
	Persuasion	2	People are encouraged to agree or give consent to decisions.
	Information	1	Participants are informed of decisions and operate out of decisions and guidelines established on their behalf.

six, seven, and eight are levels of authentic participation. Levels one, two and three are more like straw participation. We may argue that every organization is on a journey towards eight — at present, quite rare.

These days, people know the difference between authentic and straw participation. They have seen what can happen when a small group comes up with a process for eliciting broad-based participation; where everyone, even the janitor, participates. Yet so many people still believe that this is not possible. But it is possible; straw participation has seen its day. It doesn't have to prevail any more.

Witness a provincial summit on economic development. The premier at the beginning of his term called together 120 leaders from business, unions, aboriginal organizations, and the political arena. Three open-ended questions were put to the assembly. Everyone contributed. All the ideas were synthesized in two stages and distilled into recommendations. Later in his term, the premier let it be known that he had built his policies on the outcomes of the summit.

One reason managers or decision-makers fear participation is that many tools only ask people to give ideas, without asking that they process their ideas and take responsibility for the recommendations made. Dreaming up long lists of wild ideas for someone else to decide upon or implement leads to unrealistic expectations and demands, and ultimately to disappointment, blame, and increased hopelessness. The consensus workshop method can deal with that problem, as it asks the participants to process their ideas in the "clustering" and "naming" stages, and to name their commitment in the "resolve" stage.

SHIFT TO A NEW SOCIAL STYLE

Between the rigidities of *Robert's Rules* and the lower rungs of the participation spectrum on the one hand and the world of free participation on the other, lies a chasm that has to be crossed. On one side of the chasm is an old social style. On the other side, a radical new style. In between are many image and value changes. (Figure B)

FACILITATIVE LEADERSHIP

People in many different parts of society are working to bring about this leap and transformation of style. Facilitative leadership is the linchpin of it all. This new style of leadership and management, now in its infancy, will bring about a new participatory workplace and organization, and will constantly demonstrate the possibility of a new social style of communication and engagement.

The consensus workshop method is one tool of facilitative leadership. Its use (as we shall see in Chapter 2) works towards this transformation.

The Radical Shift

The Old Style *From*	Categories	The New Style *To*
1. Truth comes from higher up 2. One perspective rules 3. Right and wrong answers 4. Group diversity is a problem	I. Perception Of People	1. Everyone has wisdom 2. Truth comes from multiple perspectives 3. Learning from every experience 4. Diversity enriches process & content
5. Analysis 6. Debate 7. Consensus = agreement 8. Create ideas for others to implement	II. Understanding of Process	5. Synthesis and Inquiry 6. Dialogue 7. Moving forward together 8. Responsible for decisions on implementation
9. Obedience to boss' orders 10. Arguing competing opinions 11. Decisions made by a few 12. Power and control games	III. Decision-Making	9. Joint commitment to the vision 10. Grasping values behind the opinions 11. Representative or direct participation in making decisions 12. Creative process & partnership rules
13. Facilitation as sundry tricks and gimmicks 14. Consultants' 'interventions 15. Trying to "fix" things 16. Old top-down management	V. Transformational Intent	13. Facilitation as a revolutionary instrument 14. Life-changing facilitation processes 15. Awakening passion, involvement, commitment 16. Facilitative leadership the new form of management

Figure B The Radical Shift

Part 1

The Basic Consensus Workshop Method

This section begins with background information on ICA's consensus workshop method, to be described in Chapters 1 and 2. If you want to know how you can use the workshop method, or where it came from, start with these two chapters.

If you are quite unfamiliar with the method, begin with Chapter 3.

If you want to begin using the method now, start with Chapter 4 and proceed to Part 2.

1

Why Use the Consensus Workshop Method?

I believe that moving from an adversarial to a dialogue stance is the
core requirement, if we are to move from co-stupidity to co-intelligence.
Robert Theobald

THOSE AWFUL MEETINGS

Without some kind of orderly process, meetings can be quite chaotic. Once Gary, a
colleague, was describing how difficult it was to have a good meeting at work:

> I have a job and a boss. I go to meetings with him occasionally. One meeting in particular, every other
> Friday morning, has been going on now for what seems like eons. At the end of the meeting, the same
> ritual takes place. Not only my boss but everyone else goes out the door saying that everything they did
> at this meeting could have been done in the last five minutes. My boss goes into a little more detail than
> that because we have a long walk from the meeting place back to our office. So every other Friday we
> leave this place and go through this same ritual, in great detail, about how everything done there could
> have been done in the last five minutes.
>
> I finally got tired of listening to it one day. I decided — I think it was just out of meanness really —
> to say, "Now suppose we take this conversation we've been having together over the last year a little bit
> further. What are the three things that a group of people needs in order to operate in their meetings
> differently from what they do now? What do they need to have?"
>
> My boss is not a particularly bright man, but I was amazed. He said, "They do not know how to
> solve problems. They can't think together." (I thought, "That is not bad.") "They can't plan. It would

be a miracle if they could simply talk one at a time. They would be far down the road towards operating as a team. They do not know how to work together as a team. Thirdly, even if they did know how, they do not want to, anyway." I was amazed.

Gary went on to describe the accustomed flow of many meetings he had been in:

The meeting opens with an irrelevant comment. Then someone either asks a question or states the nature of the problem, and someone else makes a joke about the problem. Another participant argues that what has been stated is not the problem. This is followed by a debate on the nature of the problem. Finally, the meeting decides that the originally stated problem is indeed worth discussing. Two people offer different analyses of the problem. A comment is made that both analyses are biased. Someone says that the group needs a course on teamship. Someone tells a story about a course on teamship she went to. Someone questioned the validity of that course. One alert participant suggests that they had wandered far from the problem. Someone else makes another analysis of the problem. One participant comments on how easy it is to analyse problems and how difficult to solve them. Those with analyses in hand give a spirited defence of the power of analysis. The leader of the meeting throws his pen down and stalks out of the room in disgust.

Have you been to meetings like that? We all have. They're terrible. Doyle and Straus in *How To Make Meetings Work* refer to this phenomenon as "the Multi-headed Animal Syndrome."

Gary's group is trying to do a highly complex thing — to be a team solving a problem — without any method or any respect for each other. They need a workshop method, or at least a focused conversation method (See R. Brian Stanfield: *The Art of Focused Conversation: 100 Ways to Access Group Wisdom In The Workplace*). Those who have used ICA methods, trademarked as ToP™ Technology of Participation, know that the situation just described desperately needs a workshop process that pulls out everyone's ideas on the topic, understands what each person meant, looks for similarities in the ideas from which to develop themes, and pushes these ideas to come up with a well thought through answer to the problem. The process then organizes and names the ideas — in other words it needs a consensus workshop.

INNOCENT OF PROCESS

Most managers, most people for that matter, are quite innocent of process and the concept of steps in a process. Most people do not know how to take a huge topic and break it down to its components. They don't know how to think through the parts of a process. They do not understand how to pull data from many sources into one picture. They walk into a room, and ask, "What is the winning strategy we need in this area?" and make bold to hope that the results will be worth something.

There are steps to take before asking that question. There are steps to take in asking the question, and steps to take after asking the question. Understanding the consensus workshop method is understanding process thinking.

Sam Kaner et al., in *Facilitator's Guide to Participatory Decision Making*, has this no-process story:

> A software publishing company held monthly meetings that were chaired by the chief operating officer and attended by all department managers. The managers complained that the meetings were very frustrating. "Sometimes the boss cuts off discussion after five minutes," they grumbled. "At other times he lets it run on and on. Sometimes it seems like he wants us to buy into a decision he's already made; other times he couldn't care less what we think; and then there are other times again when he wants us to figure out every little detail. It's driving us crazy!"

There is no need for such meetings. There are learnable, teachable skills and processes for orchestrating a meeting that get everyone participating and sharing their wisdom. Enter the consensus workshop method.

COMMON USES OF "WORKSHOP"

The word "workshop" has several common meanings:
- a group discussion of an issue
- a brainstorming and organizing session in a group
- a meeting that is longer than usual
- a public forum providing information or discussing an issue
- a conference where many experts give presentations
- a gathering of artists or musicians who "jam" together and discuss their work.

But in this book, workshop refers to a five-step approach:
- context the group
- brainstorm the ideas
- cluster the ideas
- name the clusters and
- resolve to implement the results

Because there are so many images of a workshop abroad, ICA has recently decided to use the phrase, "consensus workshop," to distinguish the workshop described in this book from others. We wanted to change the title of this book to reflect that, but the title, *The Workshop Book*, was already agreed on. To counteract that, we have inserted "consensus workshop" where appropriate in the text.

There is considerable misunderstanding about the nature of consensus. Most people think it means that everyone agrees. A consensus articulates the common will of the group. Consensus is a common understanding which enables a group to move forward together. Consensus is reached when all the participants are willing to move forward together, even if they do not agree on all the details.

"Consensus workshop" in this book refers to the method used by ICA (The Institute of Cultural Affairs) for more than forty years in fifty countries, to enable people, in the language of Gary's boss, to "think together," "to plan," to "work together as teams."

Outside the ICA context, brainstorming is often used in society:
- for data input
- for the random listing of ideas from anyone who has anything to say.

In the process, a brainstorm often gathers information from those who are most vocal, and then only some of the information is worked with. In addition, those who have participated often feel they don't need to do anything else: "You have our two cents' worth on the topic." For them, there is no connection between participation and implementation.

WHEN THE METHOD WORKS BEST

Jon Jenkins, in *The International Facilitators' Companion*, says that the method works best when there are real decisions to make and real problems to solve:

> A consensus workshop is a method for enabling a group to make real decisions. It works when the group shares some common concern. The more concrete the concern the better the effect of the workshop. The more pressing the need is the better the workshop. Consensus workshops enable a group to develop creative solutions to non-standard problems.

It is not effective to use a workshop to impose an idea or solution. A consensus workshop is based on those who participate in the decisions of the consensus, and those who participate in the workshop are those who implement the plan or model.

In its simplest use, imagine a group of people sitting round someone's kitchen table, "shooting the breeze." The topic shifts to the neighborhood, and the state of the streets and public spaces. Someone inevitably makes the remark, "Someone ought to do something about that." The rejoinder to this is: "We are always talking about 'someone' doing something. What about us?" At which she pulls a notepad and pencil from her purse and says, "Well, let's look at this. What could we do to improve our neighborhood?" (focus question) As answers to the question come from round the table, she notes them down (brainstorm). Then she says, "Now what are we really talking about here? Let's pull these ideas together." The group pulls 20 ideas together into five main areas: peeling paint, potholes, run-down parks, public drinking fountains that don't work, and a gang that defaces public property (clustering and naming). She then segues into a second consensus workshop with the focus question, "What can we do about these problems?" At the end of the second workshop, she says, "I'm going to type this up and get you all a copy. And when should we meet again to see who does what?"(resolve)

Broadly speaking, the consensus workshop method is used for actively involving all members of a group in:
- planning: weaving everyone's input into a practical plan
- problem solving: developing solutions
- individual or group research: channeling input into a research topic
- decision making

in order to:
1. gather their ideas
2. discern the larger patterns through dialogue
3. summarize the group's insights, and
4. come to consensus on a resolution

Planning

Consensus planning workshops can be simple or complex. Using the consensus workshop for planning may be as simple as a project team's brainstorm of the tasks that need to be done that week, pulling them together into clusters, and assigning the clusters to smaller teams of two or three. Or it may be the home grocery shopper brainstorming needed items on sticky notes, and then placing the sticky notes on a rough map of the supermarket. Or it may be somewhat more complex, such as revitalizing the City of York.

The City of York was experiencing an economic downturn, and was sensing the need for fresh blood to look at the issue of revitalizing its local economy. So, the municipal government pulled together a hand-picked team of citizens from different sectors in the area to form the Community Economic Development Advisory Committee and began meeting. It quickly became evident that no single sector could manage the economic turnaround needed After the group had initiated research and met several times, it realized it could probably move faster and go farther with the help of a professional facilitator. In 1994, the ICA entered an extended contract to work with the committee.

ICA's consultation work began with a thoroughgoing planning process for the committee and its task forces. Facilitator Duncan Holmes met fortnightly with the committee to analyse the current situation and determine its advantages and vulnerabilities. Then he led the committee through a planning process which mapped out an exciting vision of the future economy. The next step was to analyse the obstacles blocking the vision. Then the group came up with new directions which concluded with delineating the projects that the committee could undertake, with the forming of task-forces. The taskforces then proceeded to implement the action plans they had built for themselves. Finally, the taskforces came together to establish priorities, create implementing teams and plan their work for the next six months.

The outcome of all this was a cause for great excitement among the committee and beyond. First, the area had a plan for its future. As a model of participative community consultation, one committee member thought the plan to be "probably the best local plan anywhere in Canada." It demonstrated that anyone could be involved in the plan's development — any sector that was left out in the original plan was brought in as soon as they came to the group's attention.

Some of the outcomes of this planning included:
• the absorption of 200,000 square feet of industrial space
• the production of a video to market the city
• a local credit union's agreement to provide capital for new businesses
• a funding proposal for a cultural center in York.

Problem solving

Facilitator Jim Rough relates this example of problem solving for a small company:
> A group of twelve maintenance workers in a sawmill were unanimous and adamant — an additional full-time person was required to oil machinery. "It is obvious!" exclaimed the workers.

"Because that person is missing, machines break down and maintenance costs are excessive. There is no other way," they said. Their boss, worried about cost pressures, did not agree. After a conversation with their boss, they agreed to do a consensus workshop to find another way to solve the problems without further hiring. In the workshop they pulled together their ideas into a four-point plan which more than solved the problem without requiring an additional person.

1. A new oiling device that would save about 20 person-hours a week

2. Saving time through changing the kind of lubricant they'd been using

3. Using a state-funded training program for oiling and maintenance which made existing oilers more capable.

4. Changing job classifications so that the equipment operators could do much of the needed oiling.

Instead of pursuing "the only thing we can do," the group used their own creativity to break through old patterns of thinking. By solving their own problem, the group not only achieved success but also grew in competence, confidence and trust.

The workshop method can be used to come to a consensus on how to deal with a specific problem.

Architect Gae Burns worked for many years with Manitoba Housing. At one stage he was asked to design a new women's shelter. Gae did not believe it possible to do it all without consultation; he believed in asking the client, in this case the women and the board of directors, what they wanted. He used the workshop process to develop a sense of what was needed. The women already had an old shelter, so they had some idea of what would be needed in the new one. Gae got them all together and asked them to imagine what the new building looked like. Then he went around the room to get their responses. He then had them group their points together and title them to define the qualities they wanted in the shelter. Gae then went back to his office and drafted a design based on the workshop results.

Some days later he pulled the women back together to share the design. He then asked them to answer two questions, working in groups of two or three:

1. What in the design did they want to keep?
2. What was lacking in the design?

They were asked to write their responses on cards. When the group reconvened, Gae clumped the answers under each question in groups and named the clumps. On the basis of their responses, he came up with a redesign that fit the needs of the group. The consensus workshop method was instrumental in solving the problem of how the building could best meet the needs of the women and children it serves.

Sometimes a whole series of consensus workshops is required to do the necessary consensus job. ICA facilitator, Bill Staples, reports on one such situation. The newly amalgamated city of Miramichi in New Brunswick was experiencing tremendous change. The amalgamation of communities precipitated an intense dialogue on the future of the area. The closure of the Canadian Forces Base had pushed unemployment levels to a high level. The new city did not want competition with the surrounding rural area and so it empowered a steering committee to embark on a process of community economic development.

The committee wanted ICA to consult with the surrounding communities to ensure that the city and the region did not work at cross purposes. It was necessary to create a broad consensus, so that everyone could pull together behind the same plan. It had become clear that a strategic economic development plan for the region must be comprehensive and had to include grass-roots community participation.

Bill and his colleague organized community forums in each of 24 neighborhoods, towns and hamlets across the region. Each small community was guided through a vision consensus workshop, a challenges consensus workshop and a strategies consensus workshop. The planning of each community was written up and these documents, together with some participants from each community, were assembled at a central point.

Then, representatives of each community gathered with the steering committee to review the work of the 24 community forums. This cross-communities gathering of about 140 people created 17 action plans, one for each suggested strategy, along with a recommendation on the team members who should work on it.

The meetings were attended by more than 600 people, who were delighted to be able to contribute their ideas on what was needed. The then-Premier of New Brunswick, Frank McKenna, attended the plenary of 140 people, gave his commitment toward implementation, and called the whole process "a sterling example of democracy in action."

Individualized research

It should be mentioned in passing that the workshop method can be useful in individual research. A friend of mine who had never heard of this method told me the process he had used for writing his Master's dissertation.

> I thoroughly researched the topic in books, periodicals and case studies. I wrote every single item related to the topic on an eight-inch by five-inch card. Each card indicated the topic and, on the back, the source of the ideas. There were hundreds of cards. When it came time to write the dissertation, I spent a couple of afternoons sorting the cards by topic. I made a different pile for each topic. At the end of it I had ten piles. I gave each pile a name. These names became the chapter headings. I then took each pile and sorted them into chapter sections. Then I sequenced each section. I then took the Introduction pile and wrote straight from the cards putting in the connections. I did the same with the other chapters. My thesis received a very high rating.

I pointed out to him that he was using the workshop method to collect and organize his data. He was quite surprised. Of course, in the first instance, the workshop is a life method. It is the way the human mind naturally operates, so it was really not surprising. Listing, organizing and sequencing the ideas works well for most of the things we need to write, whether letters or articles, or books.

Group research

Some years ago ICA Canada conducted participatory research into social trends. The question, "What is a key trend, going on today?" was sent out to colleagues across

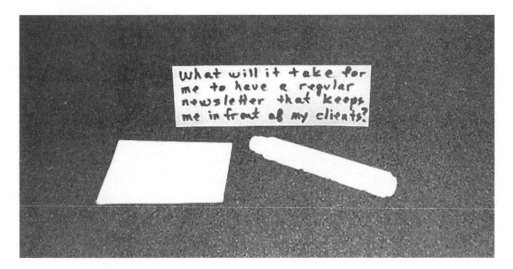

Figure 1 This workshop will use sticky notes instead of cards. The focus
question is at top of the sheet, with a pad of sticky notes and a marker.

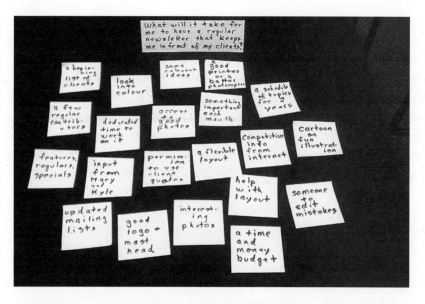

Figure 2 A newsletter editor has brainstormed a number of things he needs to produce a regular newsletter.

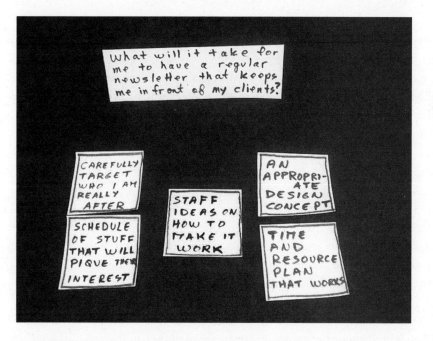

Figure 3 The editor has clustered and named the five main areas of action for publishing the newsletter regularly.

Canada over a nine-month period. The questions were sent out by e-mail, popped onto bulletin boards and online conferences, asked at dinner parties, and workshopped at several meetings of ICA Canada members, including the Annual General Meeting. Over a thousand pieces of data were collected. At the ICA Annual General Meeting, the participants took the data on cards distributed among teams of two or three people to cluster the cards and give titles to the clusters. They put the cluster titles on larger cards. The facilitator led the whole meeting in clustering these cards and putting names on them. The results went into a database, which was written up and distributed to participants. The final document was titled *21 Smoke Signals for Century XXI.*

The above section has included some large, complex examples of the practicality of the workshop process. But the reader needs to be aware that any question that can generate 15 or more answers can be a topic for a consensus workshop. For example:
- What are the qualities of a great vacation?
- What values do we need to hold in finding a new house?
- What are the qualities of an ideal spouse?
- What are the keys to effective teamwork?

(See Appendix 2)

A second, even more ambitious example of research through workshopping was the Corporate Reading Research Project. This was a research construct through which many minds, though spatially separated, could do pure research together in a specific problem area. The immediate aim of the project was to provide data for a research conference the following year. Its specific intention was to create the central database for building a multidimensional model of how society works.

The design called for the 400 staff of the Institute at that time to individually "screen" two books per month related to the processes of society for a three-month period of the year. Each book screening was reported on a common form and 1000 books were screened. It was hoped that at least 500 of these would be of real significance to the final product. With the data from these books, a research team was able to extract categories from the cards, begin clumping them in triangular sets, and finally build what are now called the Social Process Triangles.

This is an example of scientific inquiry (rather than scientific experimentation) where an overwhelming amount of evidence can be put together to discern a larger pattern that has never been seen in its totality before.

Chapter 14 describes many more applications of the consensus workshop method, but one way or another they tend to fall under these four types:
- planning
- problem solving
- research
- decision-making

Perhaps the reader is asking now, "Where did this method come from?"

Some Background

Leap on the stage to give a human meaning to the superhuman struggle.
Nikos Kazantzakis

GRADUATES OF ICA'S Group Facilitation Course often ask, with some exasperation, "But where did these methods come from?" So this chapter is for the those with a passion for sourcing.

The consensus workshop development process proceeded in an organic manner. Many sources came together as ICA staff did problem solving together.

DEVELOPMENT OF THE METHOD

I first came across the phenomenon of brainstorming in Australia somewhere round 1961, when I was doing a teacher refresher course. A speaker who had recently been on a research trip in the US introduced us to brainstorming. A question was posed and our group was instructed to shout out our ideas as they occurred to us. The instructor wrote them on a flip chart. We were told to lose our inhibitions and advised that no ideas would be judged. So we were free to shout out any ideas at all without feeling uncomfortable. We were further told that we should build on the ideas called out by other participants. The purpose was to obtain as many ideas as possible for later analysis.

As I recall, there was an immense amount of shouting. The facilitator managed to get down lots of ideas (not all of them, naturally.) At the end, we were expected to marvel at all the thoughts we had produced. We were told they would be analysed later.

At the time, it seemed a very novel idea, but inconclusive. I remember not being favorably impressed. It seemed like a lot of "sound and fury, signifying nothing." And I knew what happens with things that "get analysed later."At this stage in the development of this method, there was no way to pull all the ideas together into a synthesis. The method was exciting, but impotent. Synthesis was to come later.

Alex Osborn's "brainstorming"

My Internet research indicates that one source for the brainstorming part of the workshop method was an advertising executive by the name of Alex Osborn. In 1941 Mr. Osborn found that conventional business meetings were inhibiting the creation of new ideas and proposed some rules designed to help stimulate them. He was looking for rules which would give people the freedom of mind and action to spark off and reveal new ideas. To "think up" was originally the term he used to describe the process he developed, and that in turn came to be known as "brainstorming". He described brainstorming as "a conference technique by which a group attempts to find a solution for a specific problem by amassing all the ideas spontaneously by its members." The rules he came up with are the following:
- No criticism of ideas
- Go for large quantities of ideas
- Build on each others' ideas
- Encourage wild and exaggerated ideas

He found that when these rules were followed, a lot more ideas were created, and that a greater quantity of original ideas gave rise to a greater quality of useful ideas. Quantity produced quality.

Using these new rules, people's natural inhibitions were reduced, inhibitions which prevented them putting forward ideas which they felt might be considered "wrong" or "stupid". Osborn also found that generating "silly" ideas could spark off very useful ideas because they changed the way people thought.

The development of this original technique was considered revolutionary at the time, and since its birth in 1941, has spread throughout the world. You can read Alex Osborn's original approach in his book *Applied Imagination*.

The Delphi Process

Another possible source was the Delphi Process, originally developed in the 1950s by Olaf Helmer and Norman Dalkey, both scientists at the Rand Corporation. It served as a repetitive, consensus-building process for forecasting futures. The process unfolds like this:

1. Each member independently and anonymously writes down comments and suggestions about ways to deal with a problem or issue.
2. Ideas are compiled, reproduced, and distributed to members for observation and reaction.
3. Each member provides feedback to the entire group concerning each of the comments and proposed solutions.
4. The members reach consensus on which solution is most acceptable to the group as a whole.

This has similarities with the Osborn method, with two differences. First, it gives participants time to think up their ideas, and second, there is a degree of processing of results, in which a consensus is reached.

ICA's contribution

ICA revolutionized the brainstorming technique with the addition of gestalting, acquired from Jean Piaget's writings on gestalt psychology. ICA was studying Piaget at the time for his contribution to educational theories. The word gestalt is German, and can be a verb. It means things like organizing, or making a whole pattern out of many parts. According to Gestalt Psychology, images are perceived as a pattern or a whole rather than merely as a sum of distinct component parts. Gestalt emphasizes the tendency in the human mind towards integration, organization and cooperation.

ICA used gestalting as the third step of the consensus workshop method. Today, we are a little reluctant to use this word, since it is unfamiliar to most people. We use instead clustering and naming. But gestalting is what is going on. In front of the group may be a cluster of 10 to 20 cards. We use the steps of the gestalting process to enable a whole new creation to crawl out of the cluster of cards. The process is part rational, part intuitive. The addition of the gestalt was the equivalent of putting a Formula-1 engine into a Model T Ford. This allowed participants to make sense of their own brainstorm, rather than giving it to someone else to take away and do it for them. Consensus workshopping became a powerful instrument of formulating consensus.

ICA began using the consensus workshop regularly as a standard tool in the 1960s. As ICAs spread round the world in the late 1960s and early 70s, the workshop was the standard problem-solving tool. By then it had acquired its contexting step.

When ICA began working with corporations in the mid 70s, it applied its methods to a business seminar called Living Effectively in the New Society (LENS) course which ICA taught all over the world. It was a series of four consensus workshops — vision, contradictions, proposals and tactics — aimed at catalysing global responsibility in corporations. Later in the 70s this planning method was adapted to the holding of community consultations in less developed countries.

In the mid 80s, ICA developed training courses on the workshop and the planning methods. These courses are increasingly taught around the world to pass these methods on to future facilitators. Although "the definitive" paper on consensus workshopping was written in 1971, the art of workshopping has continued to evolve through practice ever since. Recently, the method's fifth step was named "Resolve," rather than "Consensus" or "Reflection."

THE UNIQUENESS OF THE METHOD

Not long ago, a group of ICA-trained facilitators were asked to respond to this focus question: "What is the uniqueness of the consensus workshop method?" Their answers were grouped, named and documented, using the workshop process. This is what they said.

The consensus workshop is a universal, human approach

This method will work in any management system, at any level of technology, at any time, at any place, whether in an African village or a Fortune 500 company. This method is not based on a right/wrong, good/bad dualism. It hardwires open inquiry into the process. Its inquiry is appreciative: it acknowledges the goodness of the reality it deals with. It is laden with values that fit the working requirements of most groups. This approach affirms and honors the real struggles and hopes of the participants. Rather than the application of a toolbox to a situation, it is an integrated approach to listening to reality and working with it.

The consensus workshop has a transformational intent and result

The workshop method is more than a smart methodological gimmick. Its intent is transformation. It enables participants to let go of their individualized views and allows them to expand with the help of the new insights and syntheses in the workshop. It allows people to respect and understand each person's viewpoint and experience. It allows them to see the relationship between their own and others' ideas. In so doing, it opens up and broadens their own thinking, so everyone walks away with a different perspective on reality. This morale-building approach works to bring about depth change in participants' perspectives on life. It empowers groups to listen to each other, go beyond their anger and irritation to pool their wisdom towards making decisions and building models for the future. The proactiveness built into the method breeds proactiveness and commitment in the group. It sidesteps debate and defending viewpoints, and allows participants to contribute to a larger solution, transforming their relationship to each other from protagonist to co-creator.

The consensus workshop is transparent, human methodology

The approach is contentless: the content is supplied by the group. The method serves and protects the interests and concerns of the group. It does not merely serve the needs of the client. The approach works with analysis and synthesis, but with a bias towards synthesis. The use of the workshop method is grounded and flexible. It is built on how the mind of the human being works. The facilitator remains neutral and transparent to the process. The workshop does not promote experts, but teams in action. The method is not fancy, but effective. It produces sustainable results. It operates with very high ethical standards.

The consensus workshop has high respect for the group and its wisdom

The method has built into it an unusually high degree of respect for the group and the individuals in it. Participants have been known to say, "We have never done planning this way before — we have never had respect like this before." The multifaceted approach relies on an integrated understanding of group dynamics: it understands how groups think. The method avoids manipulating the group. It acknowledges that all participants have wisdom. The method elicits radical participation. All input is acknowledged, honored and received. In the workshop, the interests of the group are protected and explored. In the process, the group becomes clear on its real limits, so that it can be creative within them. The workshop's inclusive consensus-building allows groups to have a high degree of consciousness in relation to the decisions it makes.

THE IMPACT OF THE METHOD

A few years ago, we asked a question of a group of students who had been through a week of ToP™ methods training at Northern College in Timmins, Ontario. They brainstormed out their answers to the question. Subsequently the data was grouped, named and again documented. This is what they said about participatory methods. Perhaps these impacts are also part of the uniqueness of the methods. Here they are:

The consensus workshop can heal power imbalances

The methods take down the walls between stakeholders. The methods enable an audience to move from a divisive and negative inward focus to a more harmonious positive focus directed at the future. When people experience ToP™ workshops, they make the journey from protecting their own turf to developing a common group focus. The workshops have been known to heal long-term conflict.

The consensus method enables shared power

The method enables people to really listen to each other. People come to the table as equals and experience the power that is at the centre of the table. When the process is taken back home and used, there is also an indirect impact on the community.

It increases the effective use of resources

One result of using the consensus workshop is that meetings produce decisions, speed up results and finish on time. It stops the endless cycle of planning. It marries planning with doing. Even more practically, workshop techniques help give credibility to get funding for process work in organizations. At the same time, their use has been known to reduce customer error in making purchases and, in companies, to reduce costs associated with products and service

It provides a structured process for progress

Without a method that recognizes all contributions from a group, individuals often sit on information because they do not trust the group to honor it. The process used often serves to jumble ideas for greater confusion rather than greater understanding. Consensus workshop methods have the ability to pool and pull participants' information together into larger, more information-rich patterns. They also provide a forum for recognizing the progress that has been made in an organization. In addition, strong focus questions increase the chances for success in solving issues, while a clear methodological framework guides "hot" discussions past the possibility of group meltdown. "Heat" is deftly channeled into light to yield a creative consensus.

It distills high-quality outcomes

The consensus workshop method has a reputation for cutting through participants' propensities for speechifying to create clear decisions with quality, commitment and satisfaction. Decisions made are more effective and targeted, and have more commitment behind them.

It gives the group courage to risk

Consensus workshops engage a group. They allow cultures to be bridged, and different views to be appreciated. Deeper levels of conflict are exposed as the process intensifies. Courage is reborn in the group, the courage to do something new. Such courage is the forerunner of unleashing potential and creativity. Such an environment allows wisdom to emerge. It elicits a depth and wealth of unknown knowledge, and, with it, the group conviction of "can do."

It sustains trust and commitment to the process and results

In the consensus workshop approach, the way in which the facilitator acknowledges and affirms all participant responses without judgment means that participation is greatly enhanced. In the process, competition disappears. The group comes to own both the problem and the solution. It is free to develop a group consensus. A side product is the understanding of the relationship between personal, community and organizational growth.

It releases freedom for personal transformation

One value-added dimension of a group's exposure to workshops is an openness toward growth and development. Participants experience somehow that the territory of personal development and interpersonal growth is objectified for them. They experience personal transformation at the intellectual and emotional levels. One can witness a group moving from despair to hope, turning on like light bulbs. But more even than all that is an increased commitment to improve the current situation.

Well, after all that, if you are reading this chapter by chapter, maybe you're ready to dip into the method itself.

3

THE CONSENSUS WORKSHOP
AS LIFE METHOD

_____

The major question is not whether to use participation, but how.
Laura Spencer

ICA/ToP™ METHODS

Over the years, the Institute of Cultural Affairs has created a pot pourri of methods —
study methods, training methods, organizational and community methods — to better
carry out its work. Some examples of its methods are:

Group methods
- The focused conversation method for group dialogue
- The workshop method for group planning or consensus making
- The strategic planning method for long-term organizational planning
- Meeting orchestration for designing and leading meetings
- Study methods
- Charting for individual study
- Seminar method for group study
- Presentation method for preparing and delivering presentations
- Curriculum building method for planning training or education programs
- Corporate writing method enabling the group preparation of a document

Community methods
• Historical review for rehearsing the history of a community or organization
• Trends analysis for analysing key shifts in the times
• Gridding the local community to provide an image of the parts of the community

Personal growth methods
• Reflecting on the day
• Keeping a journal
• Surface-to-depth reflection
• Spirit conversations

FOUR PHASES

All these methods have four levels, because they are all built from the same surface-to-depth pattern.

The four phases of the pattern go something like this:

Phase I deals with the objective stuff of life: what is there, what we are up against, the empirical factual data, the situational parameters, the internal and external observable data. The focused conversation method calls this stage the objective phase. The workshop method names it the brainstorm.

Phase II moves to a sensing of the internal relationship to the content of Phase I. It covers interior reactions, initial intuitive responses, emotional states or tones, feelings, memories and associations, a precognitive sense of things. It is a second "take" on the data. The focused conversation method names this phase the reflective. In the workshop method it is the clustering, the association of ideas.

Phase III relates to the data from Phases I and II. It sifts the data from those two levels for clues to meaning, insight and learning. It concerns itself with the significance of the data for the individual or group. In the focused conversation method, this step is referred to as the interpretive. In the workshop method it is the naming of the data clusters.

Phase IV gathers up the data from the previous three phases and projects it forward into the future. It generates the implications or new directions flowing from the data. It is often a process of stating the consensus, decision, implementation and action. It is the "so what?" phase. The focused conversation method refers to this phase as the decisional step. In the consensus workshop method, this is the resolve step.

It is always important, when dealing with ICA's methods, to distinguish between the surface-to-depth four-phase process and the set of steps peculiar to the specific method. The four-phase pattern can take myriad forms in which specific methods may not be recognizable. The consultant may go in and ask these questions:

1. How would we describe the situation here?
2. How are people responding to the situation?
3. What options are open to us?
4. What do we need to do?

Or this set:

1. What's the problem we are encountering?
2. What previous experiences are we reminded of?
3. What approaches might we take to solving this problem?
4. What might be the first steps? Who should be responsible for doing those steps?

Or these questions:

1. What does this team really want to produce?
2. What is blocking that vision?
3. What strategies would unblock the vision?
4. What specific actions are needed to implement those strategies?

These questions all follow the same template.

So, what are the steps of the consensus workshop method? What follows is a description of the method in very broad brushstrokes. The following chapters will describe the parts of the method in much greater specificity.

AN EXAMPLE OF THE METHOD IN ACTION

Let's join the survivor mentality for a few moments and imagine that a dozen of us are marooned on a deserted Pacific island. Our flying boat has crash-landed on a reef. We have crawled out of the wreckage, swum or helped each other to shore, and found ourselves basically unhurt, except for a few scratches. You, yes you, decide to take charge, to play the role of leader. What do you do? Well, you can stand up like a general and start issuing commands. This is likely to get the group murmuring. "Who in the heck does he think he is?" "What says she knows what's best to do?" — And they're right.

The alternative is to lead the group in a workshop.

Step 1: Context

You summon the group, and get them to sit on the ground in a circle around you. You say something like: "Now folks, we're in a bit of a jam. We're on this island together, and it seems there's no way to get off it. If we all pull together as a team we can survive this experience. We don't know if anyone has any idea we are here, so we have to fend for ourselves, and presume we are going to be here for some time. It's no use bemoaning our situation. We have to figure out a way to deal with it. We have to do it all — there is no one beside us to lean on. So let's see what we have to do. I want everyone to think of two or three things that have to be done towards our survival as a group."

This step is covered in more detail in Chapter 5.

Step 2: Brainstorm

Individuals brainstorm. The leader says, "Take a minute and think, and then I'll try to write some notes in the sand to register what we have said." You wait for two or three minutes then say, "OK, let's hear what we've come up with. I'm going to go round the circle, beginning with Eliza. Eliza, what's one action we need to take?"

Answers come forth. You write a note on each one in the sand. Here is what the group brainstormed:

1. Explore the island.
2. Look for water.
3. Look for food.
4. Check out the trees for fruit.
5. Survey the plane wreckage for usable supplies.
6. Look at the plane site for luggage lying round.
7. Build a signal fire.
8. Find a place where we can build a shelter.
9. Make a list of our collective resources.
10. Make a list of daily tasks that will need assignments
11. Make a plan of how to map the island.
12. Ensure we keep our spirits up.

Suddenly people become aware that there is more to do than those actions expressed in their own ideas.

This step is covered in much more detail in Chapter 6.

Step 3: Clustering the ideas

Then you read through the list aloud to the group, and ask, "Now, what have we got here? What are some of the threads?"

One says, well there are items related to exploration. Someone else says, "Yes two kinds of exploration: the wreckage site and the island. "Looking for water and food" says someone else. "Building a signal fire and building a shelter" are related," says one of the men. "Listing personal resources, making assignments and keeping our spirits up" have to do with daily sustenance."

This step is covered in greater detail in Chapter 7.

Step 4: Naming the clusters of ideas

You say: "Folks, looks like we have four clusters of ideas here: 1. exploration; 2. food and water; 3. fire and shelter; and 4. daily sustenance."

This step is covered in greater detail in Chapter 8.

Step 5: Symbolizing the resolve

You are now at the implementation stage. So you say, "Well, it's good to have the big picture. Now it looks like we need teams of people for each of these tasks. Each one of us needs to be on a team. Who will be on the exploration team? The fire and shelter team?" And so on…

Then you lead the group in a little reflection that confirms their resolve to carry out the plan.
- Let's hear again the names of the clusters. Raise hands for who is in each one.
- Someone in each cluster say what your tasks are.
- What about these tasks will be relatively easy?
- What will be more difficult?
- What will we need to take special care about as we do these tasks?
- What different situation will we be in by the end of the day?

You say, "Let's begin. Let's go to our tasks and report back to this spot when the sun is going down. Each team, take some of the bananas we found for lunch."

This step is covered in greater detail in Chapter 9.

That was a workshop.

FIVE STEPS

The example above is the workshop method at its most elementary, where it is more like a life method than a facilitator's tool. The basic five steps of the method are presented below as baldly as possible. Subsequent chapters will flesh out the steps and deal with some of the subtleties.

1. The context sets the stage for what is to follow. It calls the group to attention. It outlines the process and the timeline for the workshop. It explains the product and the outcome. It highlights the focus question.

2. Brainstorming the ideas gathers all relevant data from the group and puts it in front of them.

3. Clustering the ideas develops clusters of ideas and puts similar items of data together into related clusters. (Figure 4)

4. Naming gives each cluster of ideas a name. Larger clusters or sub-clusters are identified and given names. The result is a comprehensive picture of the ordered relationship of all ideas generated in the workshop.

5. Resolving confirms the group's commitment to the decisions they have made and moves it to action. The leader reads through the named clusters out loud and then holds a discussion to reflect on the workshop, using focused conversation questions. Finally the group decides on the next steps, and how they will document the workshop results. (Figure 5)

Now, if we want to ask about the long and the short of the method, this chapter was about the "short" of it. The "long" of it is what comes next in Chapter 4 and Part 2.

4

TWO APPROACHES TO THE CONSENSUS WORKSHOP

The question a facilitator faces is how to get the whole group sitting in the room, and the whole system they represent to act interdependently.
Peter Senge

THERE ARE TWO main approaches in the use of the workshop method: the "cards" approach and the "flip-chart" approach. The latter is primarily used with small groups, say from three to ten people. It will be dealt with separately in this chapter. The "cards" approach is used in larger groups or for more extended processes, or it can be used by individuals, or by a very small group around a table using sticky notes or small pieces of paper. The movement of similar cards closer together allows visual clues to enhance the capacity to see patterns of meaning.

This process has become greatly refined over the years. In recent years facilitators have discovered that the business of enabling a group to generate and process ideas is both an art and a science. This chapter deals more with the science aspects. Later chapters will describe the art.

THE CARDS APPROACH

Why the cards approach? According to Laura Spencer:

The card technique saves time. Participants can record their data and ideas on the cards simultaneously, rather than waiting for the leader to write out each item on a flip chart or chalkboard. The card technique allows the brainstorm data to be ordered and re-ordered easily. The technique generally affords clearer viewing of relationships among ideas with data on moveable cards, rather than in lists. Then again, the card technique facilitates the ordering process and often improves the quality of the names given to groups of data.

There are five major steps in the workshop method. The first is the context.

Step 1. The context sets the stage for what is to follow. It calls the group to attention. It outlines the process and the timeline for the workshop. It explains the product and the outcome. It highlights the focus question.

In the context, the facilitator:
1. names the topic of the workshop
2. says why this topic is important to this group at this time
3. describes the workshop process
4. delineates the product of the workshop
5. spells out how the product will be used
6. clarifies the allotment of time
7. lays out the assumptions behind the process
8. outlines the role of the facilitator and
9. defines the focus question.

Let's look at each of these in turn.

1. Naming the topic
This is basic clarification. For example, "This is a vision workshop. In this workshop we want to state as vividly as we can what we want to see happening in this organization five years from now."

2. Saying why the topic is important
We remind the group of the importance of the topic for their work and the organization. For example: "As this organization goes through the changes involved in this merger, it is crucial that each part of the organization operate with a common vision created by all of us."

3. Describing the process
This step takes the group through the five steps of the workshop. It may be helpful to use a picture of the process (Figure 4), such as:

- context
- brainstorming
- clustering
- naming
- resolving

Figure 4 A graphic may also be drawn on the whiteboard at this point,
or displayed as wall décor, to do the same explanatory job.

The facilitator says something like this: "First, we will be doing some individual work to clarify our own thinking. We'll be working in small groups to share our ideas with others. You'll put your ideas on cards, which we will get up on the wall, and work with to discern our answer to this focus question."

4. Delineating the product

This step gives participants a picture of the product they are aiming at: "At the conclusion of this workshop you will have a table that holds your five-year vision." Or, "After the workshop you will receive a document with paragraphs on each aspect of the vision. This will be combined with the vision statements from the other departments to form an integrated vision for the whole organization."

5. Spelling out how the product will be used

This is an important step. If the workshop is about naming staff core competencies, the facilitator might say, "In this workshop we are going to name the core competencies for the jobs in our department. This will be used by the human resources division in hiring new people."

At this point, the facilitator can remind participants that each will get a copy of the workshop results — it won't be a document for management only; it will not get pigeonholed in someone's office.

Steps four and five are often combined in one sentence, e.g., "After this workshop you'll have a chart that holds your five-year vision that will be used by Human Resources in hiring new people. The director will take our recommendations and make a decison"

6. Clarifying the allotment of time
Here, the leader gives everyone a clear understanding of available time: "We have two and a half hours to do this workshop. We aim to be finished by the time you usually go home."

7. Laying out the assumptions
The leader needs to name or create the working assumptions, which remain in place for the course of the workshop. For example,
- Everyone has wisdom.
- Everyone's wisdom is needed for the wisest result.
- There are no wrong answers.
- The whole is greater than the sum of the parts.
- Everyone will have the opportunity to hear and be heard.

8. Outlining the role of the facilitator
Here the workshop leader makes it very clear that the facilitator's job is not to be some kind of expert, but to enable the process, keep it on track, and intensify the dialogue among participants.

9. Defining the focus question
The leader states the aim of the workshop, and explains how the focus question was decided upon. Begin by writing the focus question on a flip chart page, and placing it on the wall so everyone can see it. It remains there throughout the brainstorm, enabling each participant to refer to it. It serves as a reference point throughout the session. Some workshop leaders highlight the question by drawing a circle round it on the board or flip chart.

Step 2: Brainstorming the ideas gathers all relevant data from the group and puts it in front of them.

1. Ensure understanding of the question
You can ensure the focus question is understood by saying what the focus question is not

about. Suppose the focus question for the workshop is: "What can we do to help our team function more effectively?"

- This question is not about how to get our organization to function better.
- It is not about how to increase our puppy love for each other.
- It is not about how to have fun at lunch hour.
- It is not about expanding our task.
- It is about how to get this team to function better.

The point is to make sure everyone understands the question.

2. Seeding the brainstorm

Providing the participants with a few examples of appropriate responses will trigger other ideas. Give some examples of the kind of responses needed to prime the pump of the group. Seed the brainstorm by adding specifics to the question. You may give some examples. For example, if the workshop is about improving the workplace ambience, you could say: "Think of specifics like meetings, team activities, communication, team tasks." Be careful not to limit the brainstorm too much. You want as much creativity as possible within the basic constraints of the situation.

3. Brainstorm individually

Give participants in the group time to do their own individual thinking. Tell them there are no wrong answers.

4. Selecting best ideas

Ask participants to put a star beside their own three to five best ideas before beginning to share.

5. Brainstorming in teams

Have the group move into small teams of two or three people to process their ideas. If the group is large, say 40 people or over, the teams will be larger and each team may need someone to guide the process. Team members share their ideas among themselves

Pass out cards to the teams and instruct them to put their best ideas on cards, using one card per idea and printing boldly. You may put up "hint cards" on the wall to guide how the team writes on the cards: "One idea per card; "Big bold letters;" "3 to 5 words per card;" "Specific and concrete;" "Preserve diversity of idea, but eliminate overlap."

6. Group brainstorming

In the first round of group brainstorming, the facilitator asks small teams to select a number of their clearest ideas. Those in teams discuss which of their ideas are the clearest.

The whole group is called to attention again. Now the leader calls for the cards: "Each group, send up front two or three cards that are clearest." The facilitator takes the cards, shuffles them. He takes one card, shows it to the group, reads it out and places it on the wall.

For the second round of group brainstorming, the leader says, "Each group, send one or two that are very different. The facilitator again takes the cards, shuffles them, reads them out one by one and places them on the wall.

Step 3: Clustering the ideas develops clusters of ideas and puts similar items of data together into related categories.

In practice, it is difficult to separate the group brainstorming step from the ideas-grouping step, since one flows into the other. Grouping is enabling the group to discover new relationships among the ideas. (Figure 5)

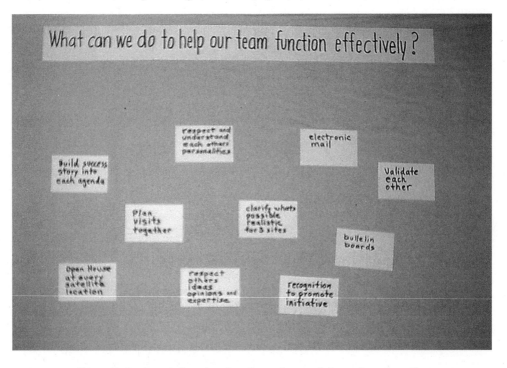

Figure 5 Cards are being placed on the wall some distance down from the focus question but randomly across the space.

1. First Round: pairing the ideas

After 15 to 20 cards are on the wall, the workshop leader asks the group to locate two cards that point to similar answers to the focus question. The leader places them next to each other and puts a symbol next to them to identify the cluster. (Figure 6)

2. Second round: different

Then the leader instructs the group to find another pair similar to each other but different from the first pair. Others are similarly created.

Get four or five pairs created in this way. (Figure 7)

After four to five pairs are created, other cards may be added to pairs. If people are not sure where a card goes, let it sit till later.

Even if a cluster has only one item, if it is quite different from the rest, it stands on its own.

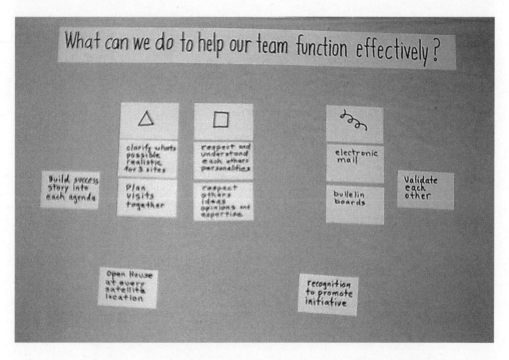

Figure 6 Here three sets of pairs have been chosen by participants and placed next to each other with symbols at the top.

3. Third round: cards that don't fit

The leader asks for all the cards that don't fit the established clusters. These are read out one by one and placed on the wall. They are then discussed and added to the appropriate cluster or used to form a new cluster.

4. Fourth round: marked cards that do fit

Groups are asked to mark cards with the symbol of the group they best illuminate, and send them up. The facilitator reads them out and places them in the cluster indicated. All the cards are now related to one of the clusters. (Figure 8)

Step 4: Naming the clusters

The challenge here is to extract the essence of a particular cluster and put a name on it. It is important for everyone to realize that the name of the cluster is one answer to the focus question.

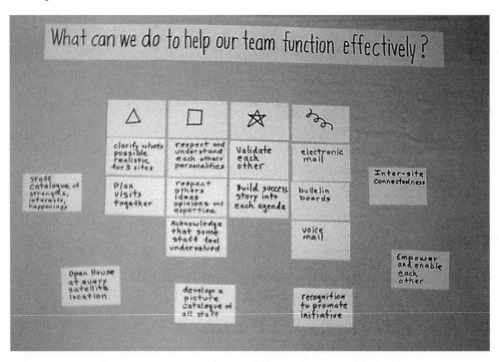

Figure 7 Here four pairs have been created and additional data placed under two of the pairs. Unclustered data remains on the periphery of the columns. More columns have to be created before they will find a good fit.

Select a cluster that is relatively clear and easy to work with. Most often this will be the largest cluster.

1. Read cluster cards
Read all the cards in the cluster aloud

2. Key words
Ask: what are key words in this cluster?

3. Discuss
Discuss the cluster for clarity and insight. Ask: what is this cluster about? What is the main idea here? Take time to explore different possibilities, then work with those until there is a common understanding of what the insight behind this grouping is.

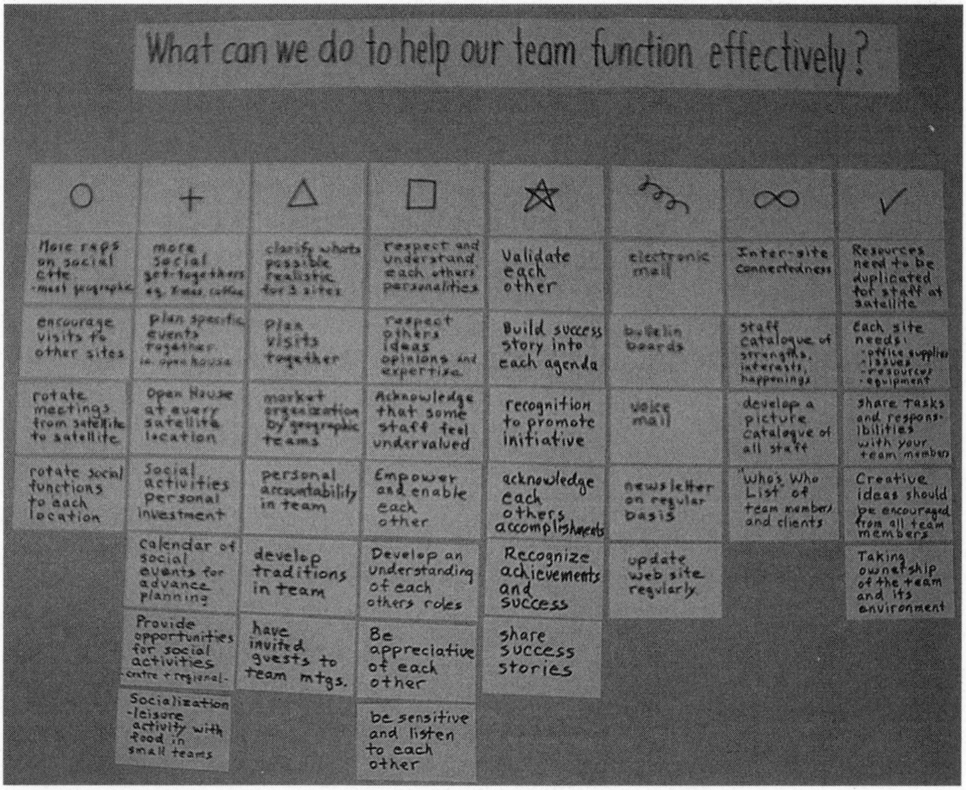

Figure 8 Note how the eight columns of data have been clustered under the symbols. The columns have not yet been named.

4. Name the cluster

Name the cluster. Ask participants to summarize the insight in a word or phrase. Ask for a few trial names, putting together insights from two or three people. Give a suggestion for the grammatical form of the name that will answer the focus question, e.g. "juicy adjective, noun or verb and object of the action" Write the name on a card and put it up on the wall.

Repeat this process for each cluster. (Figure 9)

Step 5. Symbolizing the resolve

1. A reflective conversation

A reflection on the content begins with reading aloud the title cards, continues by obtaining the group's reactions to the various cards, delineates any breakthroughs, and tests the group's degree of commitment to the results.

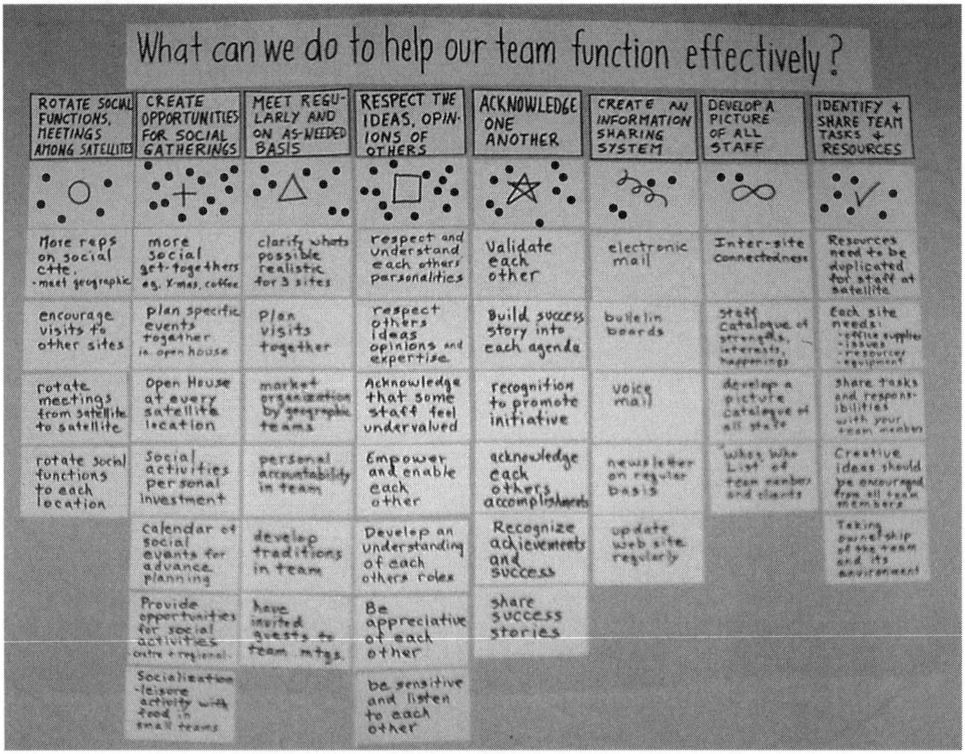

Figure 9 Here, all the columns have been named. The names are placed over the symbols, and under the focus question.

2. Documentation and Follow-up

The first level of documentation is to copy the data from the wall verbatim into a table or outline on paper. That page is then reproduced (whenever possible before people leave the room), so that participants have a record of their work, in their own words. This reassures people that their voices have indeed been heard and taken seriously.

After the workshop the documentation can be finessed with graphics and layout. It is critical to remain as true as possible to the product of the group.

Another way is to present the workshop content in a chart in which each column holds the content of an idea cluster. The table that follows documented a workshop conducted in a hospital. (Figure 10)

Creating a well-documented report provides something that can be used for future reference. (See Chapter 9 for more specifics on documentation.)

THE FLIP CHART APPROACH

The flip chart approach is best used in informal situations with small groups — where there are no more than 15 to 20 answers to the question. If there are more than that, the process becomes difficult to manage with this approach. It is also used in on-line workshops, or with overhead projectors.

Jo Nelson tells what can happen in a flip chart workshop with a lot more than 20 answers:

> Once I had a group of 25 passionate activists, all devoted to their own positions. We tried to do a flip chart method on a simple topic. They wanted it "quick and dirty." They refused to stop with 25 ideas, and filled several flipchart pages with over 40 items. They were unable to see connections between their ideas, and argued endlessly. The "quick and dirty" workshop took three hours. Immediately after this workshop we did another on a more difficult topic, using cards, and the group did the whole workshop in an hour. Their propensity to see differences rather than similarities was strengthened by the flip chart method, where their eyes had to jump around the list to find similar items. The card method allowed patterns of similarity to visibly emerge as they worked, which strengthened their capacity to construct patterns.

Step 1: Context the group

You start with the context. The context sets parameters. The focus question is the one question to which everyone brainstorms answers.

District Health Council **Multi Service Agency Consultation**					
	Board Composition Options				
		Central Recommendation			
Services Under One Umbrella	Selected Representative Board	One MSA	Plan Strategic Phasing	Elected Board	Thinking Outside The Box
Site locations consider existing facilities, i.e., information offices, community care. Max. services under 1 umbrella	Governance / representational membership: geography consumer groups provider groups. Consumers should be represented on governance board Establish provider's advisory council 1 board elected: 8 municipalities DHC special skills (lawyer, finance, etc.) Need for advisory committees in local areas	1 MSA 1 board with sites 1 MSA Board & sites to reflect community needs Prefer option #1 1 MSA focus on overall implemen-tation Re-evaluate in future Avoid admin. costs Majority voted for option 1 with certain changes Option 1 preferred (over 2) with changes	Mechanics for implementation Facts and figures on budgets Implementation planning team Interim board of providers Need an ongoing evaluation Relook at legislation. What if government changes? Ongoing evaluation of process Phase in services; series of amalgamations. Expand current home care program. Human resources, unionization costs/ agenda	Elected board best for accountability Board elected from public Elected board Elected board for: funding, community awareness and input	Be creative; let go of conceptual blocks Option: Federation of current agencies (some) central

Figure 10 Charts like this one can compress the results of a workshop on one page, while still showing how everyone's data is included.

Print the question on the flip chart.

On a separate sheet, write ground rules or working assumptions, such as:
1. Everyone has wisdom
2. We need everyone's wisdom for the wisest result
3. There are no wrong answers
4. The whole is greater than the sum of its parts
5. Everyone will have the opportunity to hear and be heard

Attach that sheet to the wall, and let it be there for the duration of the workshop.

Step 2: Brainstorm the ideas

Ask individuals to write down as many answers to the questions as they can think of. Tell them not to judge their answers, but to let the flow of creativity go unimpeded. Tell them to trust their own creativity. Suggest they note their insights in phrases of three to four words. Ask individuals to put a star beside their two best responses.

Ask each person in order for one of the starred responses. List the individual responses one under the other on the flip chart. Number the items as they go up. Ask for the other starred responses and write them on the flip chart. Ask the group for all its other ideas and get them up. It has been found that the flip chart process works best with around 15 to 20 ideas, but that should not limit getting out all the group's answers. If the number of ideas goes much above 20, it would be better to use the cards approach. (Figure 11)

Why do we record ideas on a flip chart?

Facilitators write ideas on the flip chart so people in the group can interact with them. It acknowledges the ideas and the contributor. It allows people to participate, because seeing the ideas provides a visual stimulus for thinking. This is very important for people who tend to be more visually oriented. Writing an idea on a flip chart also separates the idea from the person who contributed it. That idea now belongs to the whole group. Surrendering the idea allows the group to establish ownership of it. Recording the ideas for future use and reference is also important. People can take notes, or a fast keyboarder can capture thoughts as they are spoken. For most groups, the flip chart is the tool that is most accessible.

Some facilitators use alternating marker colors — green, blue, purple — when writing up ideas to distinguish them more clearly. This can be helpful, but don't get carried away.

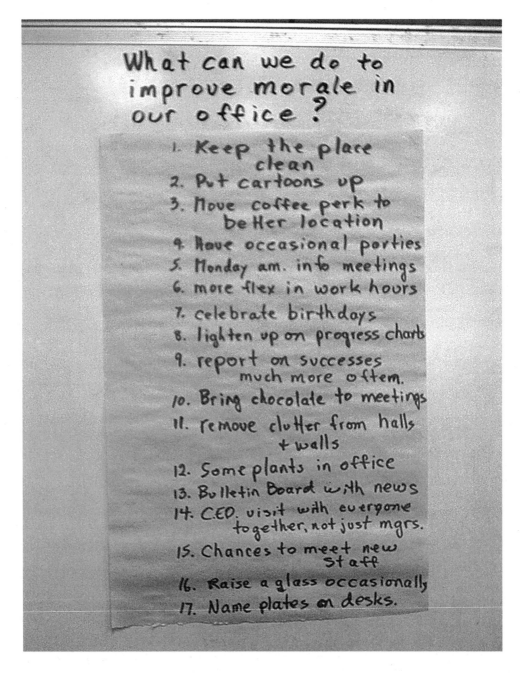

Figure 11 Fifteen to twenty items of data have been brainstormed and written on the flip chart.

The main thing is to get the ideas onto the flip chart as clearly as possible.

When printing the ideas on the flip chart, it is important to use the person's own words. If someone's idea is expressed as "High mileage per gallon," to write "Gas guzzling" on the flip chart won't do, although the facilitator might think his expression is more imaginative. The facilitator should write "High mileage per gallon."

On the other hand, some comments can be summarized a little. However, if the facilitator gets into the habit of editing every idea for conciseness or better, he is liable to get some flak from participants, and rightly so.

One ICA mentor got a call from a participant who had been in a flip chart workshop. "I can see that this method can work," she said, "but in our workshop everyone got very angry. I could see that the method wasn't the problem. Why did everybody get angry?" When the mentor asked for more detail, it emerged that the facilitator had not written people's own words on the flip chart. She had restated the ideas in her own words, and had not written down everyone's idea. The group suspected that she was writing down only what she wanted to hear, not what they had to say, and their distrust erupted in anger. The workshop was a disaster.

As we shall see later, in Part 3, the facilitator is a servant to the group's ideas, not an editor.

It is important to get out all the ideas. For this purpose it is important to have a creative way to deal with those who want to monopolize the process (more on this later). One facilitator writes:

> When I begin any session, I point out that everyone's thoughts are valuable and needed for the best results. After a context and the focus question, I give the participants time to write down their own answers before they speak. I also try to give an example of the kind of responses that we're looking for. On the first question, it helps to get one response from each person. This tends to make subsequent participation easier. Then I open the brainstorm to anyone in the group. I make it a point to acknowledge participants' ideas respectfully, because this encourages everyone to participate. It seems a truism that the first level of participation is about getting ideas out and enabling people to actually hear each other.

Step 3: Cluster the ideas

Ask the group to look at the list and find pairs of items that are similar answers to the focus question.

Tell the group that if they have questions about clarity to ask, or if they disagree with a pairing, to say so. Let the owner of the item do the explaining.

Identify four to five pairs of similar items. Use a different symbol to identify each pair.

Dissuade participants from categorizing ideas. "This pair is about economic development. That pair is about civil society." This pre-judges the cluster before all the data is in. (Figure 12)

After identifying five to six readily identifiable pairs, determine the best fit of the remaining items. You may also develop new clusters as you work with the remaining items. Ask the group to notice how the clusters grow and change as more ideas are added. (Figure 13)

Step 4: Name the idea clusters

In naming, you discern the consensus. The focused conversation method can be used here to look at cluster. For example:

Write the symbols you have used on a flip chart and ask the group to identify what is similar about these ideas.
  • Read all the items aloud with the first symbol
  • What are the key words you heard in the ideas as I read them?
  • As you see these items, what is the theme here?
  • What is the main connection between these ideas?
  • How would you name this cluster as an answer to the focus question?

Wait until the group indicates consensus, then write down the title or name beside the symbol. Repeat the process for each grouping. (Figure 14)

You may need to give the following lecturette on consensus, since most people think that consensus means that everyone agrees.
    "Consensus does not necessarily mean that everyone agrees, it means that everyone can go with a decision or proposal for the sake of moving forward. Words can never hold meaning perfectly — they just need to hold enough of it to go forward."

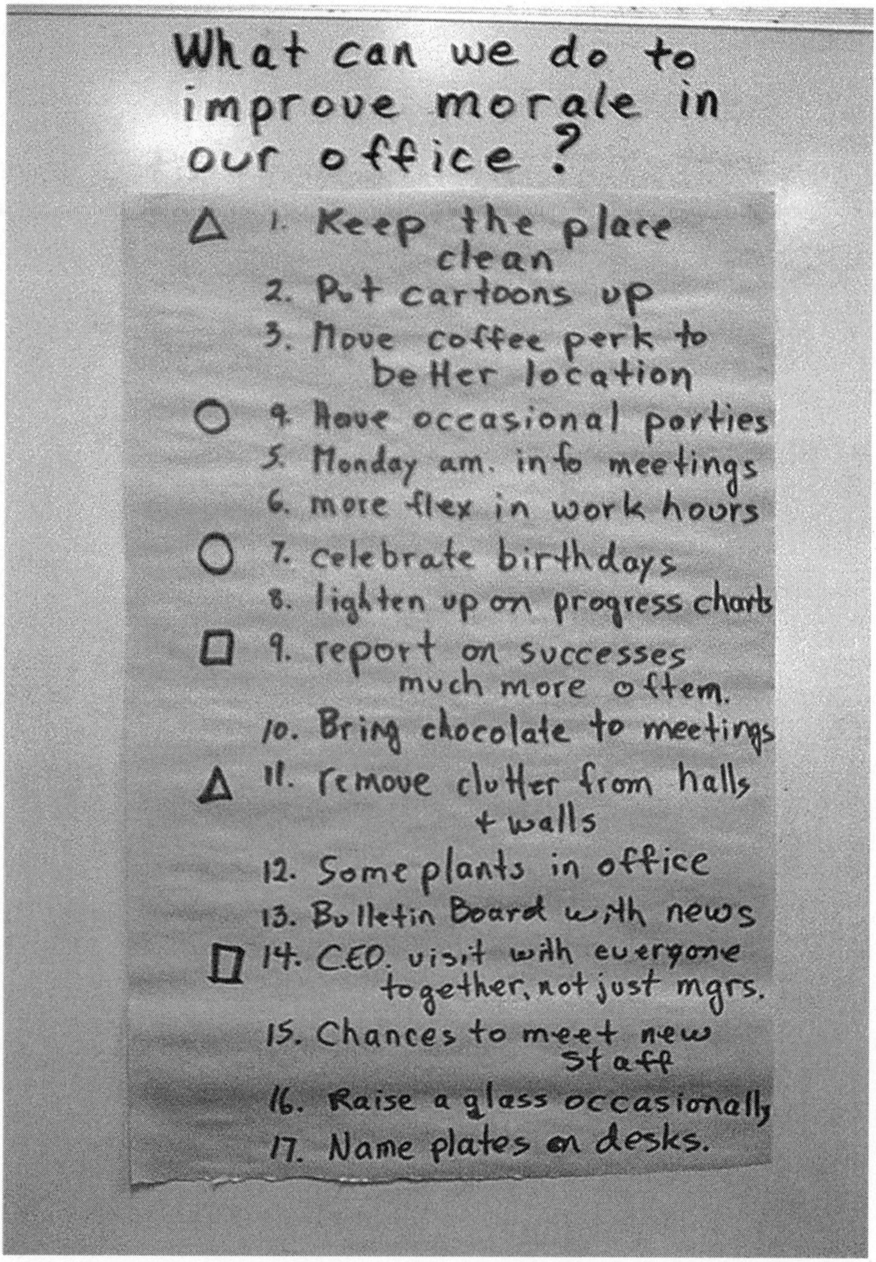

What can we do to improve morale in our office?

△ 1. Keep the place clean
2. Put cartoons up
3. Move coffee perk to better location
○ 4. Have occasional parties
5. Monday a.m. info meetings
6. more flex in work hours
○ 7. celebrate birthdays
8. lighten up on progress charts
□ 9. report on successes much more often.
10. Bring chocolate to meetings
△ 11. remove clutter from halls + walls
12. Some plants in office
13. Bulletin Board with news
□ 14. CEO. visit with everyone together, not just mgrs.
15. Chances to meet new staff
16. Raise a glass occasionally
17. Name plates on desks.

Figure 12 Note the formation of three different pairs, with more to come.

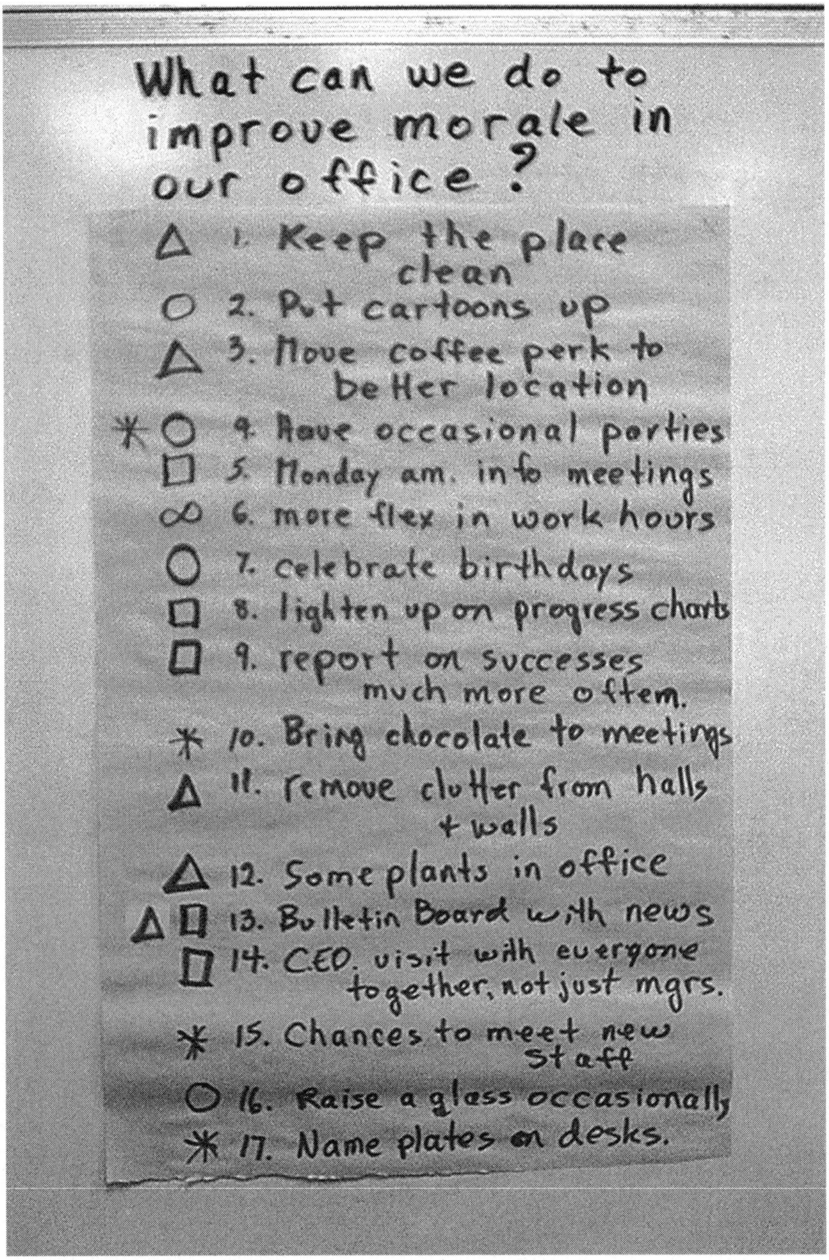

What can we do to improve morale in our office?

△ 1. Keep the place clean
○ 2. Put cartoons up
△ 3. Move coffee perk to better location
＊○ 4. Have occasional parties
□ 5. Monday am. info meetings
∞ 6. more flex in work hours
○ 7. celebrate birthdays
□ 8. lighten up on progress charts
□ 9. report on successes much more often.
＊ 10. Bring chocolate to meetings
△ 11. remove clutter from halls + walls
△ 12. Some plants in office
△□ 13. Bulletin Board with news
□ 14. CEO. visit with everyone together, not just mgrs.
＊ 15. Chances to meet new staff
○ 16. Raise a glass occasionally
＊ 17. Name plates on desks.

Figure 13 All the data has been grouped into five sets of ideas. Note that items 4 and 13 on the list have been given two symbols. At this point the group did not decide which group these items belonged to.

Step 5: Symbolizing the resolve

There are two main parts to this step, which puts a capstone on the whole process.
1. Reflecting as a group on the process and the results.
2. Documenting the results

1. Group reflection

A reflection on the content begins with reading aloud the title cards, continues by getting the reactions of the group to the various cards, delineates any breakthroughs, and tests the group's degree of commitment to the results. (See Step 5 in "The Cards Approach.")

2. Documenting the results

One way to do this is through prose statements, or paragraphs on each cluster, pulling together the ideas on the cards in that cluster. Documentation can also be done in outline form, especially relevant for a flip chart workshop. (See Chapter 9 for greater detail.)

Another way is to present the workshop content in tables using either method, where each column holds the content of an idea cluster. Figure 15 shows a table documenting a workshop conducted for a hospital.

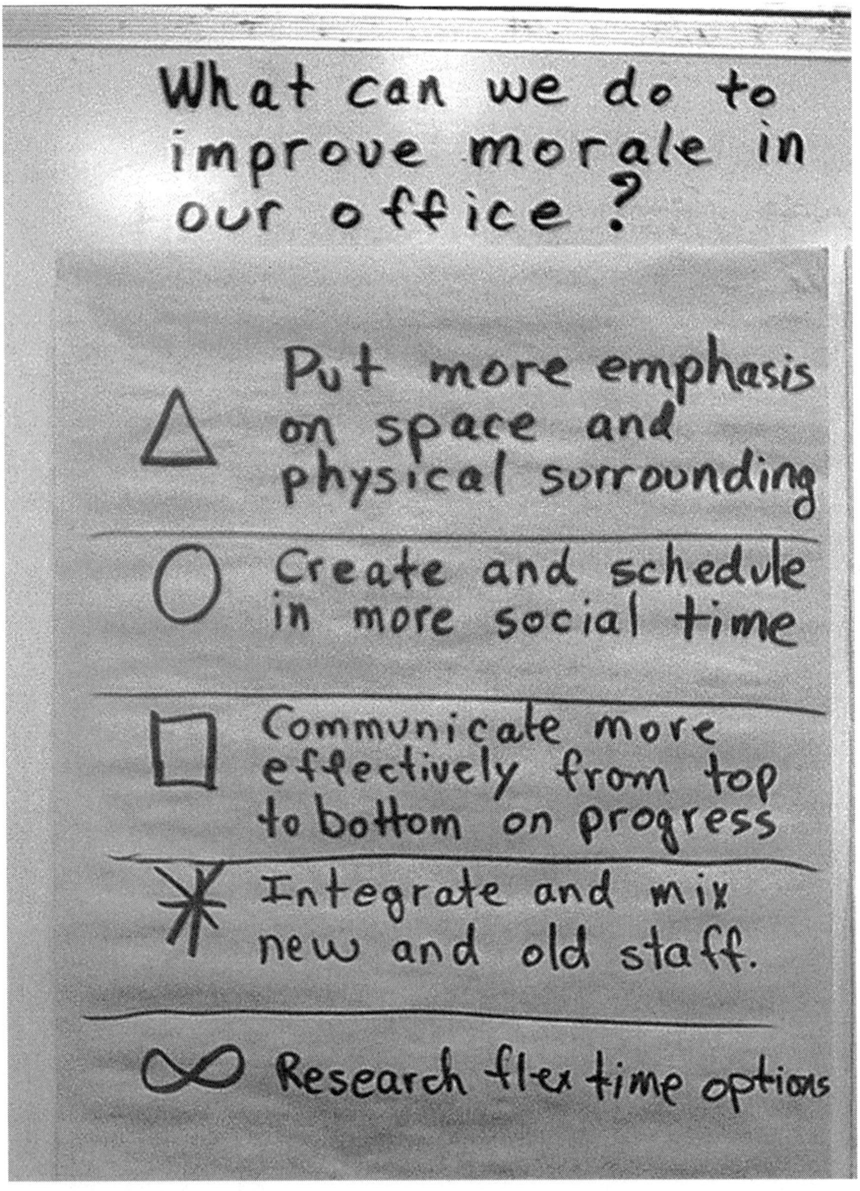

What can we do to improve morale in our office?

△ Put more emphasis on space and physical surrounding

○ Create and schedule in more social time

▢ Communicate more effectively from top to bottom on progress

✳ Integrate and mix new and old staff.

∞ Research flex time options

Figure 14 All clusters have been named. An additional prioritizing procedure has been added in the resolve.

What can we do to help teams function well within the hospital?							
Support shared responsibility	**Maintain regular effective meeting schedules**	**Build and support team strength**	**Acknowledge and advertise team accomplish-ments & successes**	**Build team identity**	**Develop clear focused goals for each team**	**Create a fun atmosphere**	**Orientation for all team members**
Rotating roles of team players. Shared responsibility of team roles Assessment of members' strengths and utilization of those skills Training for necessary skills Regular pre-scheduled meetings with rotating leader Flexibility of facilitators	Regular meeting of time and place Physical team area Better distribution of meeting minutes, communication Consistent meetings	Include participation by using working assumptions Maintain a safe environment Give praise, encouragement and support to each other Listen Encourage team members to be open to new ideas and change Check-in and provide support for completion of tasks Time to express struggles and successes Support creativity	Celebrate accomplishments Have 'team months' to identify success Monthly feature a team in newsletter Create excitement about potential accomplish-ments Team up meeting dates and information sharing dates Celebrate team's successes Sharing information with other teams Not reinventing the wheel Not working at cross purposes Promote ourselves	Team building activities and get-togethers Create team identity, colors Create a symbol, visual to identify teams High-profile approach	Develop team mandates Goals and mandate of team Clearer team-developed action goals Clearer team purpose and vision developed by the team members Relate team projects to hospital plans Follow through with ideas Help focus teams by identifying set goals Tasks concrete, and action plans relevant to team members	Try to include something fun at meetings Make it fun Each team sponsor a monthly event Incorporate social activities in team meetings Formal and informal sessions	Develop a complete orientation for new members Orientation for new team players, review goals regularly Create full book on teams Listing names and photos of team members Create a better understanding of the CQI process within the team Make sure people know what team there are on

Figure 15

Part 2

The Finer Points
of the Consensus Workshop

This section of the book provides detailed procedures for each step of the method. ICA facilitators have done many thousands of consensus workshops over the years. From the pooled experience of many workshop leaders, the method has gained sophistication and depth.

The next five chapters explore each step of a workshop in fine detail, not for the sake of finicky perfectionism, but to help facilitators make the most of the methods, to enhance group participation, and reach the best possible results. This section will also tell you why these procedures are necessary and how to avoid some of the most common mistakes.

For those who learn more visually, the ToP™ video may help with this section. It is available from ICA Associates Inc.

5

THE CONTEXT:
ORIENTING THE GROUP

In the context, you look at the sweep of history in which this consensus
workshop arises, the contemporary world in which you find yourself, the
particular life issues that impact the group, and the situation in which the
workshop arises.

Ecumenical Institute: 1971: "Workshopping Methods"

THE CONTEXT SETS the direction for a consensus workshop. A group of people
assembling for a workshop is often not ready for the focus that a workshop demands. There
may be dozens of concerns in the air. Some want clarification on what the boss really said in
yesterday's meeting. There are rumors of Christmas bonuses. Some are fretful because they
didn't manage to call home to check the pot roast. The sales folk are punching their cell
phones, each attempting to clinch deals before the meeting starts. Some are complaining
about the coffee. Others are swapping stories about their kids. This group has to be focused.

The first job of the workshop facilitator is to bring everyone to attention, to focus the
group on one focal point — this consensus workshop and its topic. In other words, the
facilitator has to corral the minds of the group. Or to use another metaphor, the leader
has to get everyone's mind in the same ballpark.

The context is not provided only at the beginning of a workshop. It's also needed before
each major step and for most procedures. So each step of the consensus workshop needs

a context:
1. The Context context
2. The Brainstorm context
3. The Clustering context
4. The Naming context
5. The Resolve context

With experience, facilitators learn some of the common traps and mistakes they can expect when groups of people meet to solve problems. With contexts, a facilitator can forestall them, before they arise. Contexts help participants to understand the whys and hows of workshop procedures. In short, the context is a device that sets the stage for quality responses to the focus question. Setting the context saves a great deal of time and makes all the difference in the workshop product. The context is crucial to firing up the group's imagination and directing it toward ideas that are relevant to the topic. In the context, the facilitator executes nine procedures:
1. Name the topic of the consensus workshop
2. Say why this topic is important to this group at this time
3. Briefly describe the consensus workshop process
4. Name the product
5. Say how the product will be used
6. Clarify the allotment of time
7. Spell out the assumptions behind the workshop method
8. Delineate the role of the facilitator.
9. Highlight the focus question.

Let's look at each of these in turn.

Procedure 1: Naming the topic

Clarify what the consensus workshop is about. For example, "This is a vision workshop. In this workshop we want to state, in as vivid terms as possible, what we want to see happen in this organization in the next five years."

The context also names the dimensions of the topic. For instance, picking up from the previous example, "This workshop is about your hopes and dreams for the organization. It has nothing to do with complaints. It is not about strategic directions. It is not about what you think the boss' vision is. It's about your vision."

Here the topic is also set in the context of past and future work. For example, "In our planning time last quarter, we focused on the marketing; in this quarter's planning, we will emphasize sales, and in the next quarter, we will work on customer service."

Procedure 2: Saying why the topic is important

Lay out for the group why you have asked them to stop phoning, typing, checking on the pot roast, faxing, e-mailing, planning, dealing with customers, and the rest of it, to spend the next however many hours to get said their practical vision. To those who are embroiled up to their armpits in the nitty gritty of any organization, this can seem as if they have landed on the moon, so they will certainly need a context for why. For example, "This workshop is the first in a series we will be holding throughout the organization to get input from all employees on the direction of each department for the next five years. Management thinks your presence in this workshop is so important that it has taken you off customer service for the afternoon, so you can contribute your input."

Explain here how the workshop was arrived at, as well. If the workshop is about expediting customer service, the leader might say: "The customer service supervisor was talking with the manager about recent complaints. They thought it would be best to consult with the customer service staff about how to resolve these problems."

When the importance of the topic has been clarified, those around the table can concentrate on coming up with creative answers, rather than wondering why on earth they're talking about this, who blabbed to the boss, and other unhelpful ruminations. Everything is out in the open.

If time and situation permit, it is often helpful to provide the context to staff members beforehand, so that they don't have to spend time wondering "where on earth this came from." If they already know the topic, the who, when, what, why, where and how on it, they can go in to the workshop mentally prepared. Of course, if materials are sent out beforehand, they still need to be reviewed at the workshop.

Procedure 3: Describing the process

Start by naming the process: "We will be using a consensus workshop process." If the group is familiar with the process, you don't need to say anything else about it. If they are not familiar with it, add, "During this process, there will be time for individual thinking and sharing ideas in a small team. Then we will work with the ideas of the whole group."

Procedure 4: Naming the product

This step gives participants a picture of the product they are aiming at. Say, "At the conclusion of this workshop you will have a table that holds your five-year vision," or "After the workshop you will receive a document with paragraphs on each aspect of the vision this group has created."

Procedure 5: Saying how the product will be used

This is an important step. If the consensus workshop aims to name staff core competencies, say, "In this workshop we are going to name the core competencies involved in our department's work. This information will be used by our human resources department to create training courses for new hires."

At this point, remind participants that they will each receive a copy of the workshop results — it won't be a document for management only.

Procedure 6: Clarifying the allotment of time

Give everyone a clear understanding of the time available: "We have two and a half hours to do this workshop. We aim to be finished by the time you usually go home. But in case we have to extend the workshop by ten minutes or so, who would be seriously affected?" There may be someone in the group who is hypoglycemic or has a plane to catch. It is good to know this early.

In announcing the total time, take the whole event into account. If the managers want to add something (like a pep talk, or the results of a research paper) they need to be clear that the time will be lengthened as a result.

Procedure 7: Spelling out the assumptions

It's important to name the working assumptions, which will remain in place for the course of the workshop, for example:

- Everyone has wisdom.
- Everyone's wisdom is needed for the wisest result.
- There are no wrong answers.
- The whole is greater than the sum of the parts.
- Everyone will have the opportunity to hear and be heard.

(See "The Workshop Assumptions" below on page 55.)

Procedure 8: Delineating the role of the facilitator

Make it very clear that the facilitator's job is to enable the process, keep it on track, and intensify the dialogue among the participants.

Procedure 9: Highlighting the focus question

State the aim of the workshop and explain how the focus question was decided. Begin by writing the focus question on a flip chart page so that everyone can see it and keep it in plain sight throughout the brainstorm. It serves as a reference point — a guiding star — throughout the session to remind the group and the facilitator of the workshop focus. Some workshop leaders highlight the question by drawing a circle around it on the board or flipchart (Figure 18). It needs to remain in plain view throughout the workshop.

Long questions confuse people. For example, "What are the indices or indicators that can be used by both our production line and our supervisors that will deal with the problems that many of our consumers have mentioned in our last survey whose results we studied yesterday?" Participants have forgotten the first part of the question by the time they hear the last part. "What benchmarks do we need to use on our production

What are your hopes and dreams for this department for the next 5 years?

Figure 16

line?" is the real question. Ask direct and relevant questions the group can answer from their knowledge and experience. In this method the amalgam of clarity and brevity is the name of the game. See more on developing focus questions in Chapter 10.

To expand the group's thinking, ask a broad question that seeks lots of specific responses like: "What can we do to make eating in the cafeteria a positive experience?" To broaden the scope still further, suggest several sub-questions, and do a little brainstorm with the group: "What might be some sub-topics of the question?" The group might say: "The use of plants and trees, safety measures, things promoting interaction." The facilitator might add: "Places to lunch alone, splashes of color here and there, improving the variety and quantity of food, and so on."

The context does not need to be long and drawn out. It is most helpful to be concise and to the point. Ensure that the group's questions are answered in the context, so they can focus their energy on the task at hand. At the end of the context, ask if anyone has questions about the process. Answer them clearly and succinctly, perhaps repeating a part of your context or add to it.

To help the participants get a fix on the focus question, it is helpful to say what the focus question is not about. For example if the focus question is "What are the elements of our new computer marketing plan for the coming year?" say, "In focusing on this question, we are going to at least temporarily bracket discussing other issues.
- This question is not about possible new products we can develop.
- This is not about deciding new job descriptions or promotions.
- We are not talking about marketing our line of printers.
- We are not talking about marketing in the next decade or next month.
- We are talking about how we want to market computers in the next twelve months."

Having established workable clarity on the topic to brainstorm, ask the focus question. "What are the elements of a new marketing plan?"

The context can be delivered faster if flip chart pages are prepared ahead of time.

THE WORKSHOP ASSUMPTIONS

In meetings today, most of us encounter a range of problems that inhibit full participation. If these issues are not resolved, the results of the meeting may not be implemented, or the real meeting may happen after people leave the room. Behavioral patterns like these deaden participation:

- A few people monopolize the conversation.
- The majority of people say nothing.
- Participants' comments are debated and argued over — sometimes with personal innuendoes that have nothing to do with the content of the original comment.
- Participants make comments like "Oh that's just a pile of peppercorns!"
- People ask questions like "Why listen to him? He doesn't get it."
- There is the belief that a few people have the answers; but there is no evaluation of whether these people get quality results.
- Or it all gets referenced back to the boss: "They pay him the big bucks; let him come up with an answer."

This behavior is deeply ingrained in some organizations and very difficult to shift.

The workshop assumptions require respect, depth listening and honoring of each participant. They are the key to creating a more participatory, engaging workshop environment. In the workshop, you respect every idea in the same way, even the most obvious idea or the wildest. You push for clarity when you or other people are not clear what an idea means. You don't just let it slide. You allow participants to explain their ideas, rather than laying your own thinking over someone else's idea; you ask what the individual or group meant by their own ideas, not what someone else wants their ideas to mean. These working assumptions are only helpful if they're held as assumptions for everything we do.

Let's look at these assumptions one by one.

1. Everyone has wisdom.

This doesn't mean everything one says is wise, but that behind what is said is wisdom, if we will listen for it. A common assumption is that only I, or some experts, have wisdom. This sets up a dualism between the wise or learned on one side and the ignorant or "dumb"on the other. Today, we understand that there are times when the voice of the expert is badly needed, but we can never allow it to replace participants' voices. When we acknowledge that everyone has wisdom, we are more able to listen to what others are saying, knowing that their perspectives are as valuable as ours. We make a shift from using cold, critical analysis of other people's words to having an inquiring mind about every comment or idea. Thus we begin to see how each idea contributes to the whole picture. The difficulty is in believing that to be so.

2. Everyone's wisdom is needed for the wisest result.

Just as a diamond is more valuable when it is cut with more facets, what we come up with will be more valuable if we can illuminate more facets of what we are working with. This makes it imperative to hear from every participant, knowing that each person has a significant point to make. Another way to say this is that each participant has a piece of the puzzle. This is why it is important to put a hold on those who tend to monopolize the conversation. Participation builds ownership in the results of the workshop. This is also why time is given for individual thinking and listing of ideas first, so that each person can formulate ideas in response to the question.

The whole perspective is gained by looking at all the individual perspectives. A workshop is not a debate. The job is not analysis, but inquiry and synthesis.

3. There are no wrong answers.

Behind what may seem on the surface to be a wrong answer, there is wisdom. The corollary, of course, is that there are no right answers — only the best we can come up with, given our limitations. In one workshop, a participant argued with this assumption, "That's not right. There are wrong answers." The facilitator — maddeningly — agreed saying, "And that's not wrong, either." In any answer and especially for the answer assumed to be wrong, you want to push for the insight or experience behind the other person's idea. People whose ideas are accepted are more willing to listen and to let their own thinking be changed by the group's understanding of the issue or topic.

It can also help to give people a context about the art of listening. Ask them to try listening, not for "mistakes," or "dumb comments" from other participants, but to listen with curiosity as to what is going to be said next. This can help them hear the wisdom in what others are saying, rather than what they don't agree with. In active listening they can raise questions, looking for the insight behind unusual comments or ideas. Even jokes have been found to have wisdom in them.

On the radical side, real listening pushes the facilitator and participants to treat every idea with the same seriousness. No idea can be written off, for any insight could turn out to be the linchpin of an incredibly successful solution to the focus question.

4. The whole is greater than the sum of the parts.

This assumption sounds trite; however, consensus creates a larger answer that is not identical to any one participant's view, but includes the wisdom of many (the diamond image again). Compromise can be seen as smaller than the sum of its parts, consensus as larger. A puzzle picture, for example, is the sum of the puzzle pieces and their relationships. All puzzle pieces are included, or there is a hole. You could take all the blue pieces and put them in a pile and name them "blue pieces," and the same with all the other colors. But this is just the sum of the parts and nothing is created by this, only a good sorting. If you take all the blue pieces and see how they fit together — the interrelationships as well as the content of the data — you will come up with "sky" or "blue car." The picture conveys so much more than just a pile of similar pieces.

The same thing works with ideas. Suppose my family workshop is around this focus question: "What values do I need to hold in buying a house?" Among other responses, I get garden, dog, and curb for skateboarding. Just sorting them into piles would include garden and curb in the physical space cluster, but that doesn't answer the focus question, and I don't get any new insight into my values. If I put the card that says dog and the card that says garden and the card that says curb for skateboarding together, they let me see that a deeper value is "urban open space." That idea is bigger than the sum of the data on the cards. The title holds an insight that is the result of not only the content, but the relationships between the data, and that answers the focus question. Behind every idea there is a larger picture not stated in words until the relationships become visible.

5. Everyone will have the opportunity to hear and be heard.
Participants want to hear others and be heard. It means listening to others as well as making sure their own wisdom is on the table. It is all too common for participants, overly eager to share or contradict, to break in on what others are saying, often without a thought that this dishonors the colleague's contribution and deprives the group of the full insight of the idea being presented. This presupposition reminds us that "everyone's wisdom is needed for the wisest result."

We also tend to listen to the first part of an idea and judge the idea by its first ten words. This assumption that everything will be heard pushes us to listen to the whole idea. And this is especially helpful during the clustering process, when fundamentally similar ideas are being linked.

6

BRAINSTORMING: HARVESTING THE GROUP'S IDEAS

The quality of any brainstorm is determined by the seriousness
with which individuals do their own thinking.
Terry D. Bergdall

BRAINSTORMING IS STEP 2 of the workshop process. The intent of the brainstorm
step is to gather as many responses to the focus question as possible within a given time.
The chapter will delineate the brainstorm step in two ways:
1. using cards, and
2. using the flip chart.

The facilitator needs a general sense of how many ideas are needed. Some situations
require only a few ideas, while others require enough to explore a great range of
possibilities. Sometimes the participants need as many as they can generate, especially
when they want to push for creativity. Often the creative breakthrough ideas come only
after all the obvious ideas have been said.

The group has to process the ideas if they are to make a difference. As you will see,
workshop ideas are processed in several ways:
- individual clarification
- clarification in small teams by comparing and contrasting them with similar ideas
- in the clustering step, by relating them to a larger cluster of ideas
- in the naming step, by pushing for the unique insight that responds to the focus question.

The kind of brainstorming this book is talking about is significantly different from other kinds. There is a common type of brainstorming used by consultants where the concern is to generate as many ideas as possible, and then select the most creative ideas. The concern is creativity. The cream of the ideas is skimmed off and the rest discarded.

ICA brainstorming is concerned with getting all the ideas and perspectives out on the table. The built-in value is respect for people. The value is not creativity, although we want as much of that as possible. More important is to get out a lot of ideas and to get each person's perspective heard by everyone else.

As with each major step in the consensus workshop, adequate time must be spent on the context:
- to clarify what is required
- to help people feel free to contribute
- to avoid mistakes and traps
- to ensure that the participants own their ideas
- to get quality ideas
- to set up a safe environment in which people feel free to contribute.

What this means in practice is that the facilitator needs to spend more time contexting each step and each procedure than might seem reasonable.

But this emphasis on the context pays off. When people feel they understand the process and know where they are going, they feel more comfortable with the program. In this environment, they do better work.

Now for the procedures for the brainstorm step.

In the fine-point method chapters of Part 2, we will use the word step for the five major consensus workshop steps. For the sub-steps, we will use the word procedure. So the first thing you do in brainstorming will be labeled Procedure 1.

Procedure 1: Ask the question

What you do
Say, "Now, again, the focus question is: What are the key elements of our mission statement?"

HINTS

1. The reference point for this procedure is in Chapter 5, Procedure 9.
2. Keep the focus question visible for the group throughout the whole workshop for ready reference.

Procedure 2: Seed the brainstorm

HINTS

1. Warming up seems to be a prerequisite for many things in life. Cold brainstorming may not produce much creativity. It's like trying to start a car or boat when the engine is cold. In the case of brainstorming, some kind of mental warm-up is needed. If it's possible, provide the question and the context to people before the meeting so they can start assembling their ideas before they even arrive at the meeting.
2. Individual preparation and solitary thinking time increase the quantity and quality of the ideas generated in a group.

The procedure

Ask for a few examples of appropriate responses to trigger other ideas. This primes the pump of the group.

What you do

Say, "Now don't just come up with your standard responses to this question. Think widely, even wildly. By all means let's have the tested and proven ideas, but also think outside the box. Your answers need to be descriptive — more than one word, but less than a sentence.

HINTS

To stimulate creative ideas, do a mini focused conversation, or ask several "what-if" questions. For the question, "What are the key elements of our mission statement?" you could add supplementary "what-if" questions like these:
- What if you were asked to explain your organization's mission to someone from a different country?
- What if you could make the impact on society that you want to make?
- What if you had to choose only two points to make?
- What if you could make twelve points?

Telling the participants that wild, even bizarre ideas are welcome can reduce social inhibitions and give people permission to be far more creative. It is important for people to know that, in a brainstorming session, their ideas will not be judged or evaluated.

Facilitator Maureen Jenkins uses Edward de Bono's six thinking hats (from his book, *Six Thinking Hats*) as a warm-up for a brainstorm. She uses a die with the colors of the six hats, one for each side. She creates a context for each of the six hats, sometimes by role. For example, the yellow hat may be for the nightshift workers. the red hat may be for the CEO, and the blue hat for a teenage customer. She restates the focus question. Each person then shakes the die, reads out the role on the exposed side of the die, puts on that hat and says what comes to mind from that perspective. If all the hats are not covered, she asks for a volunteer to suggest ideas for the remaining hat. This device gets participants thinking outside their usual roles.

In a larger group, ask people to put on other roles. Ask them what they would do if they owned the company; if they were a shareholder; or a mailroom clerk.

Of course, these ideas do not pop up naturally in the facilitator's mind. Preparation is essential where you can work on your own contexts and clarifications. (See Chapter 10: Preparation and Design)

Procedure 3: Give time for individual thinking

The Procedure

Time for individual work is crucial. For quality ideas, beyond top-of-the-head thinking, each person must have time to generate their own ideas. Give participants a little silent time by themselves to get their ideas together before opening the question to the group at large.

What you do

Say, "Take three or four minutes individually to brainstorm your responses to the focus question. See if you can come up with six to ten different responses. Don't worry about the ideas being exact. Just let your thoughts flow."

1. Some participants will say, "Oh, I don't need any time. I know what I'm going to say." Others find that they don't know what they're going to say till they have noted it down in front of them. They have to think before talking. Any group contains a range of cognitive styles. Giving people time to think up responses allows everyone to participate on a level playing field. Participants can focus on their own ideas, rather than simply reacting to what others say. Research tells us that this simple step will increase the range of thought and enable people to come up with more ideas.

2. Two to three minutes is usually enough. People with quicksilver minds need only thirty seconds to have ten ideas ready to go. Others will need the full three minutes, and then maybe more. The facilitator should watch the participants to see who may need more time.

3. Some people may need to be given permission to turn off the internal editor of the ideas that come to mind. The facilitator can assist in this by saying something like this: "You've got a little voice in your head that wants to edit your thinking. Tell it to go have a cup of coffee. The key here is to answer the focus question by writing down everything that goes through your mind, and keep writing."

4. When working with illiterate people, instead of asking them to write down a list, you can suggest they draw a picture that holds their idea, or else make a mental list and hold the ideas in mind.

Procedure 4: Select your best idea

The Procedure
This is a quality step. It ensures that the best thinking gets into the mix. The facilitator assures participants that all their ideas will eventually be asked for. This step lets participants contribute their best ideas first.

What you do
Say, "When you are finished with your brainstorm, look back over your list and put a star beside your three best ideas."

1. In response to the direction, "select your best idea," there's always someone who asks, "Yes, but what do you mean by best?" To prevent this, you can give this direction, "Put a star beside your three best ideas—however you define that." You don't want to filter out some very good ideas. Best allows participants to make their own choice.

2. Another common question is, "Why star at all? Why not just take everything people wrote and get it up on the wall?" First, starring allows participants to look back through the free flow of their brainstorms and decide what to say in the team. This means that those who are shy have already decided what to say. It also enables each person to start the process with what they consider to be their best thinking. This process is a second reflection on the data. Some folks come up with pretty rough stuff in their individual brainstorm or in emotion-laden issues they share with their team. Asking for the best idea helps them concentrate their thinking.

Procedure 5: Brainstorm as a team

The Procedure
Divide the group into teams, where participants will discuss each other's ideas.

What you do
Say:
1. "I'm going to divide you into teams so you can share your ideas. You will find many similarities in your ideas. In your teams, remove the overlap between ideas, but keep the diversity. Read out your starred ideas first, then move on to the rest of them.
2. "At the end I will need six to eight ideas from each team.
3. "I'll give you blank cards and some markers. Place one idea on each card. Write in big bold letters so that your idea can be read from the back of the room. Use four to six words to describe your ideas. Do not use one word for your idea: one word can mean many different things. Be clear, concise and descriptive.
4. "You will have 15 minutes in your team.
5. "I will divide you into small teams and tell you what spaces your team can work in."

Divide the participants into teams and launch the team discussion.

Explain: "Each team discusses all the ideas and chooses a number of the clearest ideas, eliminating overlaps, but honoring the diversity of perspectives. (For best results you want a total of 35 to 60 cards from the whole group.)

HINTS

1. This preliminary team work allows discussion and filtering of the ideas at a level where real discussion can take place. This team work is crucial in ensuring high-quality data. It encourages the participation of the quieter people who tend to be overawed at the idea of sharing with the large group.

2. When sharing, teams do not confine their choice only to the starred ideas. They begin with them, and use the rest of the lists as needed.

3. If you have 10 to 20 people, a team will usually consist of two or three people. Actually three people is better. It makes for a greater sense of safety, since with teams of three it is more difficult to know who was the source of an idea. You also get a greater diversity of ideas in a team of three.

4. Larger groups of 20 to 60 will need teams of five to ten each. Here the facilitator may have to select people for each team, nominate leaders, and supply them with simple procedures for facilitating the team. (See Chapter 14. Using the Consensus Workshop Method with Various Group Sizes.)

5. Preserving diversity is critical at every stage. When assigning teams, take a little time to ensure diversity in the teams. For example, if all the members of a small organization are planning, it would be important to mix people from management, customer service, marketing, support and even the janitorial people in each team. Spreading men and women and different backgrounds across the teams will enrich each team. The way you structure the teams helps ensure quality results.

6. The number of ideas you ask teams to select depends on the size of the group and the number of teams. For best results, you want a total of

between 35 and 60 cards from the whole group. Divide the total number of cards you want by the number of teams. So if you want 40 cards from five teams, then each team needs to produce between seven and nine cards. Some groups will come up with a lot of ideas, some with a few. The key is to make sure you end up with enough, but not too many, cards.

Procedure 6: Team selection of ideas

The Procedure
Each team selects a number of their ideas to share with the larger group.

What you do
Say: "Next, we want to get the ideas on to cards. We are after seven to nine random but distinct ideas from each team. We are not looking for a system of ideas, or a collection of abstract categories, just particular things or actions.

"Do not confine your choice only to the starred ideas. You can begin with these, and use the rest of the lists if you need to."

HINTS

1. Don't give each team too few or too many cards. Eight to ten cards is usually about right, six may limit the quality of ideas. If you give them fifteen to twenty cards, they may fill them all and the workshop will drown in data that takes too long to process.

2. Sometimes a team wants a linked thematic set of ideas. That is a trap, because when the time to group ideas comes around, people in that team will say "Oh those ideas have to go together," which will upset the clustering process. It is important to insist on the randomness of idea selection.

3. When teams are working, it is not time for the workshop facilitator to leave the room for coffee. You need to watch the teams to make sure everyone is participating and that the round-robin procedure is working. It is all too easy for the quick-draw thinkers and the fast talkers to dominate even a small team and swamp the creativity of the shyer team members in a flood of words.

4. Watch that each team is progressing:
  - Watch that they are not stuck on one idea, but are moving to discuss them all.
  - Watch that they are getting ideas on cards using more than one word.
  - Remind them of the time they have left.
  - See that one person is not dominating the conversation.

Procedure 7: All teams put their best ideas on cards

The Procedure
Teams write each of their best ideas on a card.

What you do
Say: "Each team is going to write each of its best ideas on a card. It is important to put only one idea on each card. Write your answers on the cards in large, bold letters."

Then give an example:
I'm going to put these two cards up on the wall to help us remember: 'LARGE BOLD LETTERS' and 'ONE IDEA PER CARD'."

HINTS

1. The facilitator insists on large bold lettering, so that people at the back of the room can see them.

2. The facilitator must hold a balance at this point between giving the group enough discussion time for all the ideas, but also ensuring the ideas are written onto cards, to keep the process moving along.

3. Sometimes, participants ask, "Why all this emphasis on math — 3 to 5, 8 to 10, 35 to 60 cards? Why not get all the answers of every participant up on the wall?" Experience has shown that brainstorming everything may take days to process and misses the initial filtering (clearest ideas, most passionate ideas) which lays the foundation for the rest of the workshop. (See "Possible pitfalls" later in this chapter.)

Procedure 8: Teams prepare to present their work

At the end of the team work, ask the teams to sit together and to spread out the cards on the table (if there is one), so everyone can see all the ideas.

BRAINSTORMING USING A FLIP CHART

You can also use a flip chart rather than cards for a smaller workshop so participants can interact with the data. Writing an idea on a flip chart separates the idea from the person who said it. Each idea now belongs to all the participants.

HINTS

Writing

- Begin each page with a title or a heading.
- Write what people say. Get permission to shorten thoughts if you have to. Use key words and complete phrases to capture the meaning.
- Write in STRAIGHT UP, PLAIN, BOLD LETTERS. Use the wide tip of the marker for easier reading from the back of the room.
- Write slowly enough so that your writing is legible. Practice this.
- When writing, remember that meaning is more important than spelling.

Numbering and coloring

Number the items in sequence for ready reference, not to indicate priority. As you finish a page, put it on the wall with putty or tape.

- Using different colors alternately for each idea can make ideas easier to read. Use no more than two or three colors.
- Use strong colors — black, blue, green, brown and purple — for text. Use light colors — red, orange, pink and yellow — for highlighting. Some facilitators use only black for printing for easier reading from the back of the room. Never use light colors for printing.

Handling the pages

- A single list covering the whole width of the paper is easiest to use. Use two pages side by side if you are brainstorming two things at once, like strengths and weaknesses.

- Have a simple, effective way of handling the pages and sticking them to the wall. Post multiple pages in an orderly way for continuity of thought.
- At the end of the session, roll up the sheets in order and label them for accurate documentation.

POSSIBLE PITFALLS

There are certain places in the flip chart brainstorming step where serious mistakes can complicate the workshop:

1. Changing the wording from what the participant actually said. This dishonors the participant and deprives the group of that participant's real insight. You may think your changes clarify the idea, but, in fact, it will change the meaning. If an idea needs clarifying, ask the participant to rephrase it.

2. Not listing everyone's ideas, but only those that seem sensible to you, the facilitator. This makes you a judge and expert rather than a servant of the process. Your role is to enable others' input.

3. Skipping individual pre-thinking and listing of ideas. This can cut off the participation of those who need more time to think, and weaken the quality of the brainstorm ideas.

4. Letting people pass on participating, with "I don't have anything new." Once one participant comes up with this, it tends to spread like a plague. You need to push participants to read out something they wrote down in the individual brainstorm time. Often a similar idea may have a new twist or insight. Watch for it.

5. Not having everyone speak. Getting everyone's voice heard is a challenge. Once a person has spoken once, it is easier to speak again. Getting everyone's voice out early in the consensus workshop process makes it easier for the quiet person to contribute again.

6. Moving on without understanding what each idea means. "Could you say a word more on that?" helps ensure clarity.

THE FACILITATOR'S DISCIPLINED CLARIFICATION OF DATA

The facilitator's basic stance is that each participant has real wisdom to contribute. A piece of data may look nonsensical on the wall, but it may be only later when you come back and push for real clarity that you begin to see the insight that is behind the item. There's usually more behind it than first appears. If the idea is not clear, does not answer the question, or is inflammatory, the facilitator has to ask the participant to clarify what is behind the idea.

In one public meeting in a small community, a man proposed killing all the cats and dogs. That got a reaction from everyone. The facilitator held off the angry responses and asked the man to explain himself. He said that he was a gardener (everyone agreed he had the nicest gardens in the community) and he refused to put up a fence, as fences did not make good neighbors. He was tired of dogs and cats digging up his garden. Hence his solution: "Let's shoot 'em." Everyone agreed up to the point of shooting. As the facilitator kept pushing, it became obvious that his insight was "caring for community gardens."

So it's important to have a battery of questions ready to clarify the data, and to ensure that it all gets into the stewpot.

One of the presuppositions here is that participants have the wisdom to deal with their issues. Don't be naive about this. If a group is dealing with its own business or its own community, it's quite likely it has the wisdom to know the issues and invent the solutions. But if a group is workshopping to try to break through on some problem in cybernetics, it may well be that the needed wisdom is not sitting around that table. The brainstorming process sometimes includes the research that has to go on to get hold of all the related data that is needed. For some brainstorms, specialized knowledge may be needed from a lawyer, engineer, computer expert, or architect. With luck, an expert is available on site, or the information can be gathered beforehand. But, even without expert input, the experience of the other people concerned must be honored. Never let an expert shut down people's participation.

7

CLUSTERING IDEAS:
ORDER OUT OF CHAOS

Upon this gifted age, in its dark hour
Rains from the sky a meteoric shower
Of facts.... They lie unquestioned, uncombined.
Wisdom enough to leech us of our ill
Is daily spun, but there exists no loom
To weave it into fabric.
Edna St. Vincent Millay

THE INTENT OF CLUSTERING

A consensus workshop is not an analytical process, but a process that belongs to inquiry. The opposite of inquiry is advocacy. The advocate pleads, recommends, and pushes a specific perspective. An advocate is convinced that one position is right and seeks others who will support it. An inquirer, on the other hand, comes at a topic with an open mind and looks for a creative or viable option, or for the facts of a particular matter. Inquiry attempts to open up new ground, or get a new take on established truth.

The consensus workshop as inquiry can unleash the powers of intuition and association to see connections among ideas, connections that are not immediately obvious. It seeks a breakthrough of insight that is contained in the data but is also beyond the data. This is why for many years ICA's name for the clustering and naming process taken together was *gestalting* — a breakthrough insight that comes from many pieces of data.

Making clusters from a big mass of data

What happens when a group is confronted with a large array of ideas on a wall? Start small and begin where clarity is greatest. Here's the process.

The starting point is where participants' ideas are written on cards, which are spread out in front of them.

Procedure 1: Give a context

The context, as usual, is very important. The participants need an image of where they are going. So you say:

"We are going to put these cards on the wall in clusters based on similar answers to the focus question. Then we're going to gather some more clusters, and some more. Eventually we'll arrange all the cards in clusters, and we'll name them.

"We're going to do this in rounds. First we'll get the clearest cards up, then those you are most confident about, then the ones that are different from the previous ones. I'll ask each team for its clearest card. I'll read each card out loud, show it to you, then fix it to the wall. Next, I'll ask for the cards you are most confident about. We'll do the same with them. Then I'll ask for cards that don't fit and we'll put those up.

"While the cards are going up, we'll answer questions of clarity only. The team whose idea it was will do the answering. I'm sure you understand that it is not appropriate to argue or disagree with any card at this point. Any judgmental or editorial comments will cut off participation.

"If you see a card go up and you don't understand what it means, don't try to interpret it yourself, but ask about it right then. Don't look on this as interruption. It's really a clarification—for everyone.

"When we get enough cards up, we are going to look for pairs that go together. We will put cluster cards together that go together.

Each pair will be the beginning of a cluster. When we have four pairs, we can then add other cards to the clusters.

"We are going to use symbols at the top of the columns—a circle, plus, triangle, square, infinity symbol and so on. These symbols have no meaning in themselves, but they keep us from categorizing or tagging. They don't let us give titles to the clusters prematurely, before all the ideas are in.

"When you see an idea that goes with an existing cluster, say, 'That idea goes with the circles.' That makes it easy for me to locate the cluster. If someone says, 'That's in the circle cluster', you can look at all cards in that cluster to see if the card fits there. But if someone says, picking out one idea in the cluster, 'It's the same as marketing plan', that is the only card you would compare it to, which will limit our clusters.

"We also want to be sure that even the last card we add has the opportunity to change the group's understanding of what the cluster is about.

"So that's the process we're going to use. Let's begin."

HINTS

1. The facilitator chooses the form of clustering, whether in columns, randomly on the wall, or in a matrix.

2. Columns are an increasingly common form chosen by the facilitator because of the columns' capacity to be built into, and be part of, a table.

Procedure 2: First round of cards

You say: "Each team, send me your two clearest cards" or "Send me the two you feel most strongly about." Shuffle the cards. Hold up each card to the group. Read it aloud and place it anywhere on the wall. Put the other cards up randomly as they are read.

1. After you have read all the cards, it is good to remind the group to keep asking questions if ideas are not clear. You could say, for example, "If you are not clear on what a card means, ask and we'll have the group who wrote the card explain it to us." This keeps with the group the responsibility for asking for clarity and raising questions.

2. Do not ask, "Is this clear?" after each card.

3. If you, as facilitator, are not clear on what a card means, ask for clarity. If you don't understand why a card is being added to a cluster, ask — for your own clarification and understanding. A facilitator who does not understand the data or the clustering can no longer help the group.

Procedure 3: The Second Round

You say: "Send up one or two cards that are very different." Add these to the random placement. Keep going until you have 15 to 20 cards on the wall. Any items that do not fit the cluster can be left as single cards on the lower part of the wall, but separate from the clusters.

Procedure 4. Pairing cards

You create a pair when two cards point to a similar answer to the focus question — the same issue or the same approach.

Pairing is the first stage of forming a cluster. After 15 to 20 cards are on the wall, ask: "Where do you see pairs of ideas that point to the same issue, element, problem or characteristic?" Use the focus question to clarify the type of similarity.

Put them together and put a symbol next to them.

Tell the group that if they don't agree with this pairing, to say so and ask for clarity.

Then find another pair of cards that are similar to each other but different from the first pair, then others, placing a symbol beside each cluster.

Create four to five pairs before adding cards to the pairs. Don't do anything with cards that people are not sure about.

Insist that participants name the groups by one of the symbols, rather than by some preconceived name or title, such as "the economic group" or "the public relations cluster." Using such titles prematurely prejudges the content of the column. As more cards are grouped in a column, it may turn out to be not about economics or public relations, but something more comprehensive or quite different. It is important to allow the insight emerging in clusters to grow or change.

HINTS

1. You create four to five pairs of cards, so that participants begin to see the range of cards they've offered so far. It is very easy to see relationships between all the cards and have one big cluster. In pairing, you are teasing out the various aspects of the group's response to the focus question.

2. The leader and the group need to let go of preconceived categories and relationships. Each cluster, when finished, will form part of the final product, which answers the focus question. You place a symbol at the top of the cluster so you can refer to each column without restricting the idea to any name. Discourage naming the clusters until all cards are up.

3. You especially want to avoid referring to a column by one of the cards in the column. This has the same impact as prematurely naming the column. For example, if a card in the "square" cluster says, "Revamp the training curriculum," it is unhelpful to refer to that column as "the training column."

4. It is important to be aware that the participants' insight on clustering may be quite different from yours as the facilitator. Keep tracking in your head why people are clustering ideas the way they are doing.

5. Avoid clusters based on these approaches:
   • clustering cards with the same word in them. Deal with the whole idea, not just one or two words on the card.

- clustering cards together by cause and effect. (If you do this, then this happens.)
- clustering cards in a sequence because they seem like a series of actions. (You do this first, then that, then that.)

6. If a card fits more than one cluster, ask why it would go in each location. This helps participants understand the ideas and the clusters that are emerging. Usually one cluster emerges as the place to put the idea. If not, you may need to ask which cluster the card adds most to. You may have to write an identical card and put in in both columns.

7. Sometimes the card actually contains two ideas and needs to be rewritten so that each idea is clearly stated on a separate card.

8. The symbols have no meaning. You put a symbol with the cluster so it can be referred to without naming the idea. Discourage naming the clusters until all cards are up.

Procedure 5. The third round

Tell the teams to review their remaining cards.
1. Mark the ones that obviously fit with the appropriate symbol.
2. Pass up all the cards that don't fit.

Work with these cards as before to see if there are any that fit into existing clusters or that can create new clusters.

HINTS   Let the group decide where the cards go. This is the point in the workshop where the clusters may grow and change. The group can reduce some overlap and things will start to get clear.

Procedure 6: Fourth round

You say, "Give me the remaining cards." Put them up quickly into the clusters, respecting the wisdom of each team. Read the cards out as you put them up. Tell participants to ask if they have questions of clarity. Say, "Anyone who thinks a card belongs in a different cluster, say so." Then discuss it.

HINTS

1. If a new cluster was formed during Procedure 5, ask the teams to recheck their remaining cards to see if any now go into the new cluster.

2. A caution here: it is dangerous to move cards around after they have been placed in a cluster, unless moving creates an "aha" for the group and does not require other cards to move. Too much movement of cards can cause the whole thing to collapse. "All the king's horses and all the king's men" will never get the synthesis together again.

3. It is very important that the whole group own the decisions being made about the ideas. Some facilitators may tell the group to put symbols on their cards and come up to the front wall and put their cards wherever they fit. This is not best practice, because participants lose track of the whole and the placement is not guided by the best wisdom of the group. Nevertheless, there are times when you may deem it necessary.

4. If there is disagreement on where cards should go, you can ask questions like these:
   a. What did you mean by that card?
   b. What were you thinking about when you wrote this card?
   c. Is the card more helpful here or there? Do you want this card over here by itself?
   d. If we put it here, are we understanding what the originator meant by this card?

5. The cards are shuffled in the first two rounds so that, as they are read out, they appear to be coming from several of the groups, not just one.

6. Holding a card up before the group and reading it aloud lets all participants see and hear the idea at the same time. This step reflects the understanding that some people perceive better through hearing than sight, and vice versa. It also communicates that the idea on the card is accepted, and that it now belongs to the whole group.

7. Make sure that you initially place the cards on the wall higher than shoulder level, so that you have room later on for making clusters and adding their names in the row at the top. You can place them on the

lower half of the board or at the side. The key is to avoid moving the cards frequently as you develop clusters.

8. The number of clusters you can create has to be limited. Between six and twelve clusters is right. However, do not attempt to force ideas into a limited number of clusters.

9. Before you begin the workshop, you may want to have all the symbols up on the wall in a row at head height. If they are always placed in the same order, the workshop facilitator can know intuitively where each symbol is located. This is helpful in placing cards. It also helps you notice the non-verbal language of the group — people nodding or shaking heads, or looking quizzical, for example.

10. Demonstrating with your style of acceptance that "there are no wrong answers" encourages the group to listen to the wisdom behind the words when they don't agree with the surface expression of an idea.

11. Answer questions of clarity only. Let the team whose idea is on a card answer any questions about it. This preserves the anonymity of the one who originally contributed the idea. This is important in a situation, for example, where the boss, who is sitting at the back of the room, finds the idea offensive.

12. Judgmental or editorial comments from you or others will cut off the participation from some people. If you don't quite understand what a person meant, it is important to ask, rather than try to interpret the ideas yourself.

13. About one-third of the total number of cards should be up before clustering begins. Often you need 15 to 20 cards so it's possible to see the patterns of ideas in the cards.

14. Figure 17 shows some commonly used symbols.

15. Make sure that the symbols you use do not have a particular meaning for the group. The indirect meaning can distract from the process.

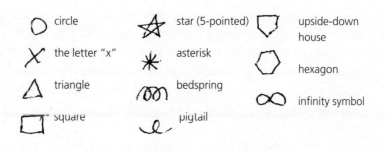

⭘ circle	⭑ star (5-pointed)	⬗ upside-down house
✗ the letter "x"	✳ asterisk	⬡ hexagon
△ triangle	bedspring	∞ infinity symbol
▢ square	pigtail	

Figure 17 Gestalt Symbols

16. Generally you want between five and nine clusters and therefore the number of symbols is between five and nine. Fewer than five, and the titles become too abstract. More than nine, and the columns begin to cluster together unhelpfully. Seven to nine clusters are most common.

TRAPS IN CLUSTERING

1. Selectiveness

Brainstorming is a common device for getting out a bunch of ideas. Many groups and consultants use it. The uniqueness of this method is in what happens to the brainstorm data after the brainstorm is over. A not uncommon practice is to pick out the best or most promising ideas, or to rank the items in the brainstorm using an array of values. What happens to the Cinderella items that are not selected? What happens to the people who contributed those ideas? Well, they don't get to dance in the participation ball. Some other time, maybe. The approach to workshops described here can hold all the data. This is the wisdom of the 4 to 6 word cards. It can all be held.

2. Categorizing

Consultants commonly pop the items under a preselected set of categories like economic, political, and cultural; or education, health and social services. Categorizing robs the uniqueness of people's ideas. Facilitator Edward S. ("Ned") Ruete has some good wisdom on this point:

> When I think back to my worst moments as a facilitator, they did not involve dealing with difficult people, or having to scrap my design in the middle of the session and start over, or lack of participation, or forgetting materials, or any of the other usual nightmares. As bad as those moments are (and I've had my share of them), they are nothing compared to the sick feeling I get when a good

exercise isn't working because I'm trying to force-fit the creative, divergent work of a bright and involved team into predetermined or hurriedly determined categories. The ideas don't fit, the participants get frustrated, and I know that the rest of the work on this project will go badly because the categories we're going to work on aren't the real categories we need to work on, and don't have a good fit of ideas in them. I feel like a charlatan, masquerading as a facilitator, but really just leading the group through a fixed process to get their buy-in, not really trying for true collaborative work products.

I just don't do this anymore. Predetermined categories, fishbone diagrams where the main "bones" are the 4 Ms (materials, maintenance, money, and manpower), planning exercises with three time-frames, process analysis based on functional departments, high-medium-low priorities: these are in my toolbox, but they stay in the box until I see that they are ideas that might help the group create its own categories.

3. Making the data "manageable"

Another inclination of facilitators, when there is a lot of data, is to somehow cut it back to manageable proportions.

One workshop exponent writes:

> The information needs to be reduced to manageable proportions. You need to find a format that will summarize the ideas for those not familiar with it.

On reading that, I think: "Oh dear! There we go again." Reducing the information to manageable proportions always raises the question of whose ideas will be omitted for the sake of "manageability." The same with summarizing the ideas. The ToP™ approach insists on using all the data and omits none. What does the poor participant think who sees her valuable insights being omitted for the sake of "manageability?"

4. Tagging

When a cluster is still forming, some participant is sure to begin talking about "the management cluster" or "the vision cluster." The use of such holding titles to refer to a cluster before all the ideas are up is known as "tagging." Some facilitators seem to find it useful. The downside is that it prematurely freezes the sense of the column. Jumping to conclusions does no honor to the wisdom of the group. It does not allow the emerging insight to grow or change. The best practice is to refer to clusters by symbols until all the cards are up.

THE CLUSTERING PRINCIPLE

It is important that everyone do the clustering by the same principle. Otherwise confusion will reign.

The clustering principle is something we use all the time in life. You look at someone's clothes closet and you can usually see a clustering principle in action. They may cluster their clothes by type of clothes (suits, shirts, pants), by season, by type of event (casual, semi-formal, formal), or by color, or by outfits.

And there are probably more ways to cluster your clothes than that. If you change your clustering principle, you end up with a different result.

In a workshop it is important to know what the clustering principle is, or some participants may cluster by cause and effect, others by items in the same geography, others by things that go well together, and so on.

Your guidepost is your focus question, which tells you what you are really looking for. The focus question ties directly back to your rational and experiential aims. (See Chapter 10: Design and Preparation of a Consensus Workshop.)

So as you prepare your workshop, ask yourself, "I will be clustering by similar what? Is it intent, element of the vision, actions, issues or type of equipment?"

We have found that there is often one easy clustering principle and another one that is a push or a stretch but holds deeper intention. You have to know where you are pushing the group. Many workshops hit a card that doesn't fit, or that seems to fit in several clusters. At this point your deeper level of preparation helps, so you know how to help the team through it.

Examples:
In a vision workshop, a typical question is "What do we want our company to be like in five years?" You then cluster ideas that point to the same element of the vision. When you need to push deeper, you ask, "Which items point to a similar intention?"

In a strategic-directions workshop, you cluster ideas with similar actions—very straightforward. On a deeper level you cluster actions that together create momentum. That is more of a stretch.

If you look at all the issues around a particular problem, you cluster by similar issues. On a deeper level, you cluster by similar root cause — that is, you group things by what is going on underneath the issue.

Thus, all the clusters should be built consistently. As you reach this point in the workshop, you need to be clear with the participants what clustering principle you will be using. Then you have to watch like a hawk that they don't begin to introduce another principle. Listen very carefully to what people are saying: "Well if we do this, then…" Oops, that is an example of grouping by cause and effect. Or if you hear, "We need to do these things in this order…" that is grouping by sequential action.

The clustering process for the facilitator is a dance of many steps: pushing for clarity yet keeping the process moving, maintaining neutrality yet straining for a quality product, enabling and affirming participation while keeping the whole group on track, and, in the midst of it all, struggling to maintain a stillness at the centre of being.

8

NAMING: ONE CONCEPT FROM MANY IDEAS

No single thing abides, but all things flow.

Fragment to fragment clings, all things thus grown

Until we know and name them

Lucretius

THIS STEP IS where you name the clusters of ideas. The essence of this step is a depth dialogue to discern the consensus of the group on the names of each cluster of data, and to develop ownership of the work. Your task as the facilitator is to coach the group in creating the titles. It is up to you to pull out the real insight that is held in all the ideas in the cluster. This is a quest for the pearls of wisdom.

The naming procedures differ according to the situations. You must decide whether there is enough time for the whole group to name each cluster, or whether small teams will have to do it. If the latter, it is important to demonstrate the naming process with at least one or two of the clusters before the small teams go to work.

Procedure 1: Give a context for the naming process

Say:
"We are now going to name each cluster. We'll begin with the largest cluster, and then move to the others. The names we will

give the clusters are not categories (like economic issues, or cultural challenges), but answers to the focus question that hold the insights hidden in all the ideas. If we turn the focus question into a statement, the cluster name completes the statement. For example, the competencies of a professional facilitator are.... The name will be three to five words that describe the concept behind all these ideas in the cluster. Try to word it as verb plus adjective plus noun, as in 'discerning group visions'."

The context helps participants see the intention of this section and how to describe the final product.

Procedure 2: Read all the cards

Select a column. Say: "I'm going to read all the cards aloud." Go ahead and read each card in the cluster.

Don't assume that participants will read the cards themselves. By reading the cards aloud, you are working on two perceptive modes — auditory and visual. You are also making sure that the group is dealing with all the ideas in the clusters — not just the ones they remember or the ones that catch their attention.

Procedure 3: Note key words

Ask: "What are the key words on these cards?"

Again you are focusing people on the data that is in front of them. Often, participants will concentrate on only one aspect of what is on the cards. As a facilitator, you want to be sure that all aspects of the data are being held.

Procedure 4: Note clues to the major idea

Ask: "What are the clues to the major idea in the cluster?"

Here there is movement from the data towards an initial synthesis.

You will probably get several different answers to this question. At this stage someone may give you the perfect name straightaway, and the participants may come out with an "Aha, that's it!" In that case, skip to Procedure 6.

Procedure 5: Pull together the insights

Ask: "Okay, so what is this cluster about?"

Have the group work with the clues to pull the insights together into a suggested name. You may go through a number of name suggestions before the right one clicks with the group. You are looking for verbal responses and nonverbal cues (a nod, for example), from the group that the name is the right one. (It often helps to point out that you are looking for a nod from more than one person.)

Tell the group that we want to kick the ideas around. We are not in a rush to the finish line. Say, "Someone else, what do you think this cluster is about? I want to see you listening to each other."

HINTS

1. Be patient. Novice facilitators tend to be afraid of this step and want to rush to decision, but you should avoid undue haste in naming. If you don't take enough time with this question, you might find that you need to repeat the procedure because there was no real consensus on the name. The job is not to get a right name in the box, but to get a consensus on the insight and then name it. Facilitator John Miller says, "This is where I sometimes find myself crouched down beside the table out of view, listening very carefully to all the conversation that is happening."

2. It's important to keep pushing the name till a common understanding is apparent. Make sure participants really struggle here. Don't let them off the hook when they come up with overly simple or pre-cooked titles. You have to remind them that naming is about what people mean, not just what they say.

Procedure 6: Check for consensus on the name

When you have a name that the group seems to agree with, ask: "Does this hold our group's insight behind all these items?" If so, write the name on a card and post it on the wall by the cluster of cards.

HINTS

1. This step is checking that the name does indeed hold the insight for the whole group. Often it helps to write the name on the card and hold it up for the participants to see, and to read it to them. Sometimes, you may need to change the name several times to come up with the right one.

2. The touchstone in the naming process is whether the name is an answer to the focus question. For example, if the focus question is "What are the constraints we have encountered in marketing in the last two quarters?" and the group comes up with a name like "not enough janitors," that won't do because that's an answer to some other focus question. It is not a constraint to marketing. But if the name came out as "old-fashioned advertising" that might be a good fit to the focus question.

3. When the group has found a good name, you can test it with questions to see if there is a real consensus. At this point you need to be on the lookout for nonverbal language. If one participant is grinding teeth, and there are several worried expressions around the room, more work is needed. Beware of trying to insert your own suggestions for naming. Get the name written on a card, hold the card up in front of the group. Ask,
   - Is it real?
   - Does it answer the focus question?
   - Does it describe what we have been talking about?
   - Does it hold the group's insight?
   If the group answers in the affirmative, draw a square round the name and put it in the heading row at the top of the cluster.

4. Some facilitators use cards of different colors for the name cards.

Procedure 7: Name the rest of the clusters

You now have a choice to make:
   a. You can repeat the process above to name each of the clusters as a whole group.
   b. You can assign clusters to small teams to name. In this case, write the process you have used on a flip chart and read it to the group. Assign a cluster to each group. Give them a card and marker for writing the name. Those teams that finish first can be given another cluster to name, as needed.

The decision whether to use option a. or option b. is sometimes based on the time you have left for the workshop. Option b. generally takes less time.

The decision may also be based on whether the group needs to do the work together to enable adequate buy-in and ownership of the results. This decision is your call, although at times the group will make their own recommendation when you tell them what you are going to do.

If participants are working in small teams, you need to watch their work and help any teams that are in trouble. Notice whether the names are fitting the pattern for the names (verb plus adjective plus noun). Be prepared to push a team for a more descriptive name, if needed.

Special process used when small teams have named the clusters

When all the titles or names are on the wall, read the cards in one column. Then read the name. Then ask:
   1. Are there questions of clarity about the title? Is anything not clear?
Continue with the other columns and ask:
   2. Are there any titles that need changing?
If a particular title is mentioned as needing some change, ask:
   3. What is your concern?
   4. What would you recommend?

If consensus on a particular title is slow in coming, you may have to go through the naming process for that column all over again with the whole group. This is important in building understanding of the names given, as well as in creating ownership of the names.

The final step of the method, dealt with in the next chapter, is symbolizing the resolve held in the group's work.

HINTS ON NAMING CLUSTERS

1. In the four questions above, some readers will recognize the focused conversation method. (See R. Brian Stanfield: *The Art of Focused Conversation*). Its use here greatly smooths the clear thinking of a group. After they have named several clusters using all four steps, they are usually capable of moving faster. If they get stuck, the group can return to the four questions (Procedure 6, Hint 3).

2. Naming clusters with the whole group is far preferable to letting the facilitator take them away and name them, then bring them back for the group's OK. A group that has developed ownership of the focus question is likely to stage a rebellion against that, even if the workshop sponsor is willing. The group has to own the product all the way. If you are pressed for time, you could get the group to name one or two together, then assign pairs or teams to name the rest of the clusters.

3. The old tension between time and quality lurks here again. The leader wants the group to create the best answer; but the group has to develop its own view. A facilitator who is overly anxious about getting a near-perfect product can make the mistake of intervening with personal ("better") ideas or language. In this workshop approach, that's a mortal sin. It removes the neutrality of the facilitator and acts as a brake on the flow of creativity.

4. On the other hand, a facilitator is responsible for moving the workshop along and watching the time. A group who has dilly-dallied about the naming process will not have kind thoughts about the facilitator if the workshop goes badly over time. Sometimes the facilitator can suggest language or a name that seems to synthesize the thinking in order to

unblock the group. If you have to do this, always preface it with: "I think I hear you saying…" Be sure to check with the group. Ask: "Is that close or do you have another suggestion?"

5. One rule of thumb in arriving at a consensus is that you never criticize or reject someone's articulation of the consensus unless you present a better one. In other words, if someone says, "I think the stars are all about "generating community involvement," the leader cannot accept responses, such as, "No they're not!" or "I disagree — I think it's all about building civil society." Ask for alternative suggestions, rather than reactions, until the group begins to respond in an affirmative way to one of them. Watch for the nods around the table. It's helpful to state this rule of thumb at the beginning of the session or as the process moves to the naming stage. You can then point out if the rule is being violated, and push for more helpful statements.

9

STEP 5: SYMBOLIZING THE RESOLVE

Far too often, participants leave interesting discussions only to have
conclusions and discussions fade into vague memories because no
tangible products were ever produced.
Terry Bergdall

A UNIVERSITY GROUP of academics hired an ICA facilitator for some strategic planning about university extension courses. The last step in the process was implementation. When asked the question about actions to take, one professor raised his hand and said in rather shocked tones, "Do you really expect us to implement these ideas, and by ourselves?" And the facilitator said, "In this paradigm, those who plan are those who implement."

The resolve step gets people used to the idea that there is follow-up to the workshop results.

In Step 5, the facilitator states the follow-up steps and pulls together a whole picture of the participants' decisions. The point is to symbolize the resolve of the group. The workshop clusters are reviewed, using the focused conversation method, and the group becomes accustomed to the idea that what they have been through is not an intellectual exercise, but something they can use or implement themselves.

The participants do need to live with and support the decisions. A conversation on implications or next steps can introduce this process.

Procedure 1: Lead a Focused Conversation

The conversation generally goes like this:

You say: "Let's look at what we've come up with here." (Read the title cards.) Then you ask:

1. What surprises you in all this?
2. What intrigues you?
3. Which one of these ideas is easiest to implement?
4. Which is hardest?
5. Which would make the most difference?
6. What are the implications of what we've said here for our group, or our work?
7. What are the next steps to be taken?

Conclusion: Jose has agreed to document the workshop. He would appreciate any help you can give.

> ♀   This conversation is the bridge between the idea and the implementation. As
> HINTS   T. S. Eliot noted,
>
> > Between the idea and the action
> > Falls the shadow.
>
> It is only too easy for a group to leave the workshop on a high note and then
> let the shadow of indecision fall upon them.

Procedure 2: Create a table to hold the consensus

A table can quickly and easily hold the total information in front of the group. The table takes the broad sweep of cards and gets them to flow into the number of columns the group fashioned. It creates a whole picture that holds balance and completeness. In creating the table, relationships between the clusters can be discussed. (See Figure 15.)

> ♀   1. A table can summarize an entire workshop on one sheet of paper. The
> HINTS   detailed minutes or background ideas are important, but a table creates an
> image, which makes the information more accessible for people. Clusters
> can be done in many different forms; for example, arranged in columns,

clustered in a circle, or in a tic-tac-toe mode. A table is only one such form, although a popular one, for summarizing workshop data.

In Figure 18, note some of the conventions in table-making.

2. Whatever final summary form you choose, this is a first step in avoiding recriminations, like this one: "The last time we did a workshop, not a thing happened afterwards. All the decisions we made were forgotten. People's projects went unsupported. These things are a waste of time!"

Create a chart to hold the consensus

A chart can quickly and easily hold the total information in front of the group. You are creating a whole picture that holds balance and completeness. In creating the chart, relationships between the clusters can be discussed (i.e. largest issue, key new action).

Sample Charts:

Shows overall
balance

Shows priorities by
number of items

Indicates forward
movement

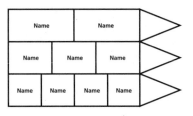

Figure 18

Procedure 3: Document and Follow-up

It is deceptively easy after the reflection part of the workshop to
bask in the wonder of the group's creativity. But 90 per cent of the
group's creativity will be lost from memory the next day, unless
the workshop is properly documented and the necessary follow-up
steps taken. Creating a well-documented report provides a
summary for future reference. Most often, the documentation step
is done by the facilitator, subsequent to the workshop. If this is not
feasible, the facilitator has to ask someone else to do it, but you
need to arrange this before the workshop begins.

HINTS   It is helpful to document the data as it showed up on the wall at the end of
the workshop. It is not for the documenter to embroider the work of the
group, although care in presenting the data always helps. Remember "the
majesty of the data."

OPTIONAL FOLLOW-UP STEPS AFTER A CONSENSUS WORKSHOP

The naming step of the consensus method creates several clusters of named data. There
are many things you can do with this type of consensus. For example, for a mission
statement, you may want to write a sentence for each column, and then arrange them
into your final mission statement. Or for a set of strategies, you may want to set up a task
force for each group of similar actions. Depending on the situation, at the end of the
workshop, you could ask the participants which option they want to pursue.

Option 1: Writing prose statements

Write sentences
Assign several people to work together to write a sentence or paragraph for each column
with the name of the column and a description of the main insight contained in the
column.

Write paragraphs
Use the data in each cluster to provide the grist of the paragraph. Ask two people per
column to write a paragraph for each column.

Use it as a table of contents

With an appropriate introduction and appendix, the workshop columns can become the Table of Contents of a research study or report. An entire chapter could be written based on the cards in each column.

Option 2: Preparing for action

Prioritize the columns

The amount of data in each column may give a preliminary idea of the priority value of each column. Use a focused conversation during the reflection step of the workshop to prioritize the columns with the group.

Set up a committee or task force

Assign a small committee or task force to each column to decide the next steps for implementing that column.

Do a workshop on some of the columns

Schedule one workshop or a series of workshops for each column in order to get more input and develop a more comprehensive picture of that grouping.

Weave the columns together to create a solution

Use the focused conversation method to make a solution that holds the information in each column.

Option 3: Creating images to hold the group's insight

Create a rational table of the columns

Engage the participants in a dialogue about the relationships among the columns and then create a table which holds the relationships clearly.

Create a picture, graphic or image to hold the consensus

Brainstorm a list of graphic images (geometric shapes, objects or artforms) and map the column titles onto the graphic images. (Figures 19 and 20)

Create a song or a poem from the work

Rewrite column titles or important words from each column into rhyming couplets or some other device. Add a tune and create a song.

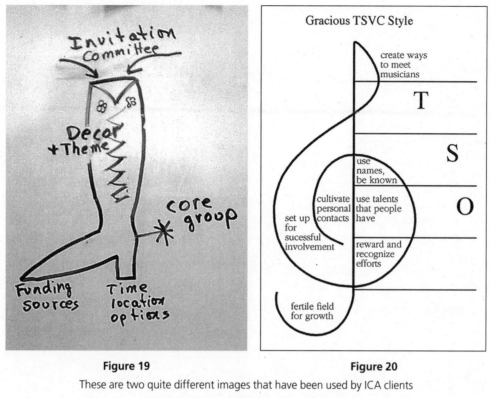

Figure 19	**Figure 20**

These are two quite different images that have been used by ICA clients
to portray the results of their workshops.

Procedure 4: Distribute the documentation

It is critical to distribute workshop results quickly. The product of
a workshop embodies the dialogue, contributions and, most
importantly, the commitment of the participants. Having the
results in participants' hands, rather than in someone's desk,
creates a sense of accomplishment for the time and energy
expended. Symbolically, it says, "This was your consensus
workshop. Here are your results." Speedy distribution of results
enables the direct move to implementation.

Needless to say, everyone who participated in the workshop
should receive a copy. If the janitor participated, he should get a
copy. Keep a copy for your own files.

Part 3

Workshop Leadership

This section describes issues of preparation and style in leading consensus workshops. It is just as essential as the chapters that deal more directly with process and procedures. Those chapters (in Part 2) deal with the science of leading a workshop. Without the procedures, a workshop is not likely to accomplish its goal.

Chapters 10 and 11 deal with the other essential — the art of workshop leadership. Chapter 12 speaks more to readers who are encountering challenges in their use of the consensus workshop method. Chapter 13 deals with establishing a total environment for the workshop using the critical elements of time, space, eventfulness, and the use of short courses.

10

DESIGN AND PREPARATION
OF A CONSENSUS WORKSHOP

Design is a complex multi-dimensional process. One doesn't just sit down
and "do it;" rather, it consists of several constituent activities often
visualized as a spiral to depict the process as a journey of successive round
trips, each incrementally shaping the destination.
Susan Wright

THERE IS A certain contemporary mindset which bridles at the idea of careful
preparation and thinking through. "Just do it!" is used as a motto by more people than
the footwear company. In this case, it seems to say, "Just go ahead and workshop — why
design, why prepare?" Suppose the builders of the Confederation Bridge between Prince
Edward Island and New Brunswick had said, "Just do it!" and went ahead putting in
pylons and trestles as they came to mind. The ice floes and wind would have had a field
day. It is true that there are occasions when you just have to go ahead with some project,
regardless of preparation. But not the consensus workshop.

What is the key to facilitating a stellar consensus workshop? A productive, satisfying
workshop depends on "the action before the action" — the amount of preparation that
goes into it and the artful design you create for it.

Most beginning workshop facilitators tend to assume that the thing they have to prepare
is the process they will use — the steps, the order of the steps, the tools to be used with

the steps and what they will say — in other words, the workshop design. But facilitators also need to think through the current situation of the group they are leading. Time also needs to be spent on honing the focus question and the product requirements. Only then can the workshop be appropriately designed and orchestrated. So, we can enumerate two major areas of preparation:

1. Assessing the group's situation
2. Designing and orchestrating the process

Again, one might well ask: Why this level of detail in preparation? Why can't I just write the question on the flip chart and get the group to have at it? What's the big deal here? The big deal is that, in facilitation, as in cooking, execution is only as good as preparation. Sun Tzu, the Chinese writer on strategy, has a famous sentence that is relevant here: "Generals win battles the night before the battle, through their preparation in the temple." It is the same with workshop facilitators. Success is assured by sufficient detailed thinking through of the total environment of the workshop — before anyone comes to the workshop. Some facilitators have been known to sweat out their preparation all night long before they go on stage. We wouldn't recommend that: a good night's sleep allows you to be more open to the group process. Nevertheless, preparation is serious stuff.

ASSESSING THE GROUP'S TECHNIQUES AND SITUATION

If you've decided to lead a consensus workshop, you need to drench yourself in background details. So, the first step in preparing a workshop has nothing to do directly with the specifics of the consensus workshop method. First, you have to understand or review the details of the organization, or group you'll be facilitating. Some questions:

What is the topic?

There are a million possible topics for a workshop. It is critical to get very clear what the topic of this workshop is: Is it human relationships, team conflict, sales strategy, marketing tactics, customer relations, staff development, suppliers, janitors' issues? And within those, what aspect does the group need to deal with? Then you need to know what the related issues are.

If the topic is contentious, you may need to spend much more time in this part of the preparation, to encourage understanding all around. But if the topic requires a very specific result that everyone can buy into, you will have to be much more meticulous in the naming — for example, creating a project implementation plan.

What is the situation? What are people concerned about?

Every consensus workshop takes place in a complex sociological context. In one workshop we did, people were passionate about getting staff-management issues prioritized, but underneath it all was a grave doubt about whether they would be empowered to deal with the issues they were prioritizing.

The facilitator knew that this kind of concern would sap a lot of the energy and motivation from the workshop. So he went to the client, to clarify her intent for the workshop. The facilitator pointed out the participants' concerns about support from the management, upon which the client said she was very interested in the results and in the group's suggestions for dealing with the issues. She said she meant to ensure that the workshop's proposals had her support, and she agreed to say so to the workshop group.

The participants felt empowered.

What are the organizational history, recent shifts and events?

It's important to know something about the organization's history, for example, how long it has been around. What major shifts has it been through, for example, the introduction of teams, employee ownership, relocation? What have been recent accomplishments and setbacks? What recent external or internal events have led up to this this workshop — a collapse of funding? Bad press? Perhaps a crisis in communication or a market that has just tripled in size? A new exciting vision within the organization? Perhaps an incredibly successful year which inspired larger goals?

In most of these instances, the workshop facilitator will need to acknowledge the climate in order to give the group permission to think about the focus question.

What is the group's past record on the topic and the current degree of consensus?

Every time this workshop topic comes up is there an explosion of feeling? Is this a hot topic? Or does it bore people to tears because they've dealt with it so many times? Is there a fair degree of consensus around the topic? Or are there several camps of opinion that must be reconciled?

What is the main bone of contention? Have they worked on the problem before? If so, what did they do? What were the results? What has happened since? This affects the context and the decision on the focus question.

If there is a history of working together and agreement, you can move much more quickly. If there is a history of dissention or acrimony, you will need to spend more time on the brainstorming step and even more time on the clustering step, so that people really do hear and understand each other. In the clustering, you will have to continually ask people to comment on various associations. In the naming step, you will have to clarify the names that people use so that participants know what the emerging consensus is. You also want to present this workshop in the context of the work already done, so that participants don't develop a sense of déjà vu.

Who are the people in the group?

This is an important question, almost a separate arena of preparation. The old pedagogical adage, "To teach John, one must first understand John" is just as true in facilitating a consensus workshop. To rephrase the adage, "To lead a workshop, one must first understand the people in it." If your task is to do a workshop for a client group, you will need to ask the client about the people in the group.

What is the current mood of the group? Are they weary? Cynical about the topic? Excited to be able to deal with one issue at last? Are they somewhat scatterbrained because of a recent crisis?

What is their attachment to solutions? Are there elements in the group who think they have a winning model — they just need to share it and people will buy in? If so, you must stress the need to listen to all perspectives. Is the group on the side of the status quo? If so, you'll need a context that stresses the importance of thinking wildly and outside the box. Or are they dying for change? In this case, you will need to remind them not to throw the baby out with the bathwater.

Is the group knowledgeable about the topic? Is the topic in their bailliwick? Or does it seem foreign to them? Will there need to be preliminary research, or a presentation? Or are they overloaded with information? If they are all knowledgeable, you can dive into brainstorming. If not, you will need to spend time on the context, maybe with presentations from people who do know the topic, or maybe a focused conversation to explore the topic and let people understand its complexity.

If people are insecure because they do not know each other very well, give them time to get better acquainted, so that they feel free to discuss things openly.

What are the cognitive and operational styles of the people? What are the main thinking and learning styles operating in the group? Are they print-oriented, highly visual, very kinesthetic, hyper-rational?

If you need movement in the room, you can plan to ask people to bring up cards to give them the chance to move around. You can ask them to change seats to do the brainstorming. Take away tables and use only chairs, if you want spontaneity and a feeling of complete openness and exposure. If you are after standard workshop process, set the room very deliberately to give the message that everything is very orderly and thought-through.

What are the keys to the way the group operates? Are they familiar with team operation? Is there a high degree of initiative in the group? Are they proactive or reactive? More intuitive or more rational? Do they operate institutionally or semi-autonomously? Is there a high degree of collaboration, or do work units keep to themselves?

Some people (e.g., company presidents or a manager) may have universal permission to get up and make astute observations at any time, and, similarly, to point out important points to the group, or comment on short cuts in the process. At other times they must be asked to follow the process to the letter, to allow for true impartiality and openness.

Be prepared to watch for people who never speak, and occasionally ask them a direct question so they can hear their own voice and feel permission to participate freely.

Without this situational examination, the workshop facilitator may do an excellent technical job on the workshop, but not a quality job for the organization.

Of course, if the consensus workshop is within your own organization, the need for this review seems less necessary, but if you do it, you will do a better job for the group.

CREATING A FOCUS QUESTION

Getting the focus question right is very important. It indicates the type of answers the group is looking for. It acts as a guide in clustering the data. The focus question enables clusters to be named in enough detail that the solution is obvious. The focus question begins with a "what." A clear question releases people to easily come up with 8 to 15 answers to the question. The questions should include a time frame, if that affects the answers.

The focus question will drive the whole workshop. It triggers the brainstorm and provides a guide for the clustering and naming. It's important to create one that both focuses the topic and elicits lateral thinking.

The subject
First identify the topic or subject. Your notes from the situational analysis will likely tell you, although this is probably fairly abstract at this point .

The time frame
There are two considerations regarding time when thinking through your focus question.

The first is how long the actual workshop will last. Usually you are given a limited time in which to do the workshop. If you have only an hour or less, you will probably be able to do a quick, intuitive workshop on an easy issue. If you have three to four hours, you can probably do some real exploration of a thornier issue.

The second consideration is the duration of the results the group needs from the workshop. Does the group need a five-year vision, so that they don't need to redo it each year? Or do they need a one-week temporary solution to a problem? This time period may be usefully made part of the focus question.

The stakeholders and participants
You need to know who will be affected by the workshop results. Staff? Management? Overseas groups? Suppliers? Certain customers? Funders? Workshop results will be wiser and more sustainable if all affected stakeholder perspectives are represented by participants. People who are a part of the process don't have to be "sold" on the results — they know their ideas are a part of the final result, and they are more likely to feel ownership of the implementation as well.

The consensus workshop aims
The Rational Aim has to do with the product of the workshop. What is the product or result needed? How will it be used? Knowing how it will be used helps clarify the form of the product you need; for example, a list of items, a set of paragraphs, a list of priorities, or one solution that involves all the elements defined.

The Experiential Aim states how you want the group to experience the workshop — how the group needs to be different at the end. If the group needs to trust each other and be inspired to move forward, the focus question and process will be very different from a situation in which the group needs to be intrigued enough about their analysis in order to meet just one more time. In general, the consensus workshop method tends to create respect and harmony.

The aims will have the most direct impact on the wording of the focus question, because the focus question elicits brainstorm of the elements of a product, and guides the clustering and naming of those elements to best produce the result that is needed.

Swirling the data

All this data and other things that you know about the group now have to swirl around in your head like a cartwheel. When it comes to rest, try writing the focus question. Most focus questions begin with a "what" question, although a few successful ones start with "how." The focus question needs to catalyze a number of specific responses from each person, within the boundaries set by the rational aim. Those specific responses, when grouped together, need to create the necessary product.

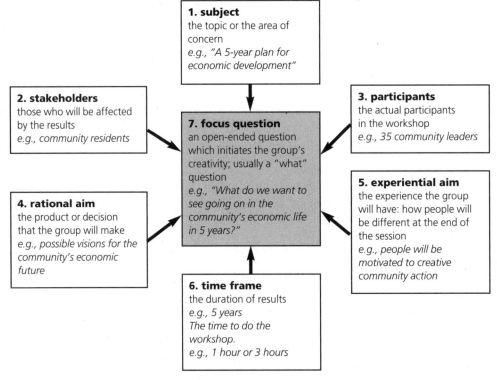

Figure 21

After choosing the best question, sit back and critique it. Run it past a colleague if possible, and see what kind of answers they give. Or imagine all the possible answers of the participants. Will the answers, when grouped with others and named, fulfill the aims? If you are not happy with your first attempt, keep trying until you have a focus question that is clear, concise, and on target. (Figure 21)

For sample focus questions see Appendix 2.

ORCHESTRATING THE PROCESS

The next step of preparation involves a fine tuning of the process. An orchestration sheet is very useful for holding at least an outline of the data below. (Figure 22)

Aims
Review the rational and experiential aims; the product, and the experience you want the group to have.

CONSENSUS WORKSHOP METHOD • FORM

FOCUS:

CONTEXT	RATIONAL AIM (S)		EXPERIENTIAL AIM (S)		RESOLVE
	BRAINSTORM	**CLUSTER**	**NAME**		

© THE CANADIAN INSTITUTE OF CULTURAL AFFAIRS 1985, 1995, 1998, 2002

Figure 22

Eventfulness

Think through what kind of icebreakers, small celebrations, and opening or closing conversations will help enliven the proceedings and make the workshop an event. Have a really good reading or story ready for when spirits fall. When is it likely the group will need to take a break? When would be a good time for them to stand up and stretch?

Technique and procedures

Think through the specific procedures that will get the job done. Is there a format you have used before that will work here? If so, where does it need to be customized? What short courses (see Chapter 13) or explanations will be needed at various points?

Movements

A good consensus workshop is like a symphony with movements, introduction, and closing. Make notes on the symphony sheet under "movements" as to which procedures, techniques, and eventfulness go in each movement, and in what sequence they go. You may need to break out a sheet for each movement, if the procedures are complex.

Time plan

You have already objectified the time you have available. Now apportion time to each of the movements and steps of the workshop, so you have a precise idea of how long you want to spend on each part of the workshop.

Opening

On the symphony sheet, note the space for "opening." Here say how you are going to launch your workshop. Will you give a context? Or do an introductory conversation, asking the group members to give their name and say one thing about themselves? Do you want to try another kind of icebreaker? What are your opening words?

Closing

Here you say how you are going to close the workshop. Will you thank the group for their hearty participation? Make assignments on documentation? Say how the workshop results will be used? Doing this step saves you from wandering on at the end, vainly trying to hit on a closing point. Write down the words you will use to close the workshop.

I remember one workshop where I floundered at the end trying to find some good closing words. I finished up thanking the students, the client, God and the Blessed Virgin Mary and then urged them to stand on guard for True North strong and free, and still kept going. Not quite as inane as that, but it was a débacle. Since then, I have written down in detail my closing words.

Personal prep

It is one thing to prepare the process. But you must also make space for personal preparation. Allow enough time to review your plans. Do a trial run of the design beforehand so you can iron out any creases. Visualize in detail what is going to happen in the event.

List all the materials and props you will need. Don't forget to prepare flip charts and other materials in advance. Create handouts that will be relevant. Inspect the room ahead of time and ensure that it meets your needs. Check to see that all logistics are covered. Inspect the site and needed resources ahead of time. If it's a card workshop, make sure you have enough cards and a way to stick them to the wall — putty, masking tape, or a sticky wall. Prepare the cards with symbols on them. See whether all the markers make a good impression. Are they toxic-free? Do a last-minute check with your client to see if anything has changed.

Rehearsing the facilitator's stance

Last, you think through ahead of time how you are going to style yourself. Not how you feel like being today, but what style is needed for the sake of the participants. Out of your previous preparation steps, what style do you need to put on that will bring off the workshop? If the group tends to stodginess, do you need to be more buoyant? Do you need more sobriety, if you know the group tends to skittishness? Does the group need a great deal of affirmation and confidence building? (More on this in the next chapter.) To stress again: the style in question here is what is needed to bring off the workshop, not how you feel on a particular day.

Without this preparation, it is like walking into the group naked — as a facilitator you are very vulnerable. But, with preparation, you can lead the workshop with more insight, more sensitivity to the group's needs, and a more disciplined approach to the whole event.

11

THE STYLE OF THE WORKSHOP FACILITATOR

Those that go searching for love

Only make manifest their own lovelessness,

And the loveless never find love,

Only the loving find love,

And they never have to seek for it.

D.H. Lawrence

THE WORKSHOP FACILITATOR'S JOB

The task of the consensus workshop facilitator is to guide a process that brings the participants' best ideas to bear on a topic, and helps them organize those ideas so they can be used.

I remember with embarrassment the first workshop I ever facilitated some thirty years ago. I had the five steps of the method down pat, but my facilitation skills were woefully undeveloped. I had my images all wrong. So I said. "The context is this…. Now we are going to brainstorm. So brainstorm away!" Nothing happened. So I said it again; "Now we are going to brainstorm. Let's brainstorm, folks!" Still nothing happened. My colleague at the back of the room was frantically trying to signal me to get the group to write down some ideas, but I had no idea about how to get them to brainstorm. I put down my marker and left my colleague to pick up the pieces of the workshop. Luckily I was working with someone who wasn't as green as I was.

I had not grasped that a facilitator has to know more than the five steps. The role is to facilitate the group's brainstorming and clustering and naming; and that requires sub-steps and ancillary processes. I needed more procedures up my sleeve to facilitate the brainstorm. It was a major embarrassment for me. (Figure 23)

Broadly speaking, there are three players in the consensus workshop:
1. The members of the group
2. The group's data on the wall, board or flip chart
3. The workshop facilitator

It might seem that the main action in a consensus workshop is the interaction between the facilitator and the group. And this is the case in many group meetings, for example in a board of directors meeting, where the main conversation is between the chair and the directors. But a consensus workshop casts the facilitator in a different role. The main interaction is between the participants and their ideas. The facilitator's role here is to enable participation, and help them process and develop their ideas.

Workshop facilitators are catalysts. Their task is to heighten the interaction between the ideas on the wall and the participants. First they get the imagination and creativity of the group operating in the same ballpark — which has to do with delivering the context. Then they lead the group in brainstorming their responses onto the wall (or flip chart). Next, they intensify the interaction between the data and the group by getting participants to create and name the clusters. At every point the facilitator is encouraging the group to deal with the ideas on the wall.

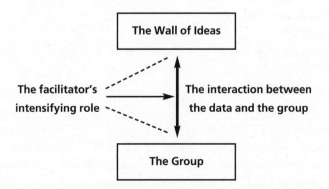

Figure 23 The Triangle of Relationships

When facilitators turn into prima donnas, focusing attention on their virtuosity, it's an unfortunate sight. The biggest mistake workshop facilitators can make is to think that they are the centre of the activity, and that the group's job is to come to terms with who the facilitator is, and not what's on the wall or flip chart. T.S. Eliot put it nicely:

Half of the harm that is done in this world

Is due to people who want to feel important.

They don't mean to do harm — the harm does not interest them.

Or they do not see it, or they justify it

Because they are absorbed in the endless struggle

To think well of themselves.

So the first thing the facilitator needs to understand is that leading is about serving the group and helping it do its job. The group is the main actor in this event. So the task of the facilitator is how best to help the group do its planning, solve its problem, create its timeline, and come to a consensus on its future vision. The facilitator's transparency is a key quality, though not easy in the practice.

Chicago facilitator Jim Troxel tells this story:

Last year I got a letter from a colleague in Indiana who is a new facilitator. I had been mentoring him as he was learning this skill. He asked, "Have you ever had the experience of having facilitated a group, and it really went great? Everyone thought you did wonderfully. They came away with much consensus and a new vision, but you felt depressed?"

I thought, "This guy is crazy. What does he mean, he felt depressed?" His question bothered me. I think it was because I identified with him a little bit more than I was willing to admit. It began to get clearer the day I picked up my wife after she had facilitated a session for the National Runaway Hotline Network. I could sense equal portions of euphoria and melancholy begin filling my wife, if you can have both of those experiences simultaneously.

I asked, "How did it go?"

She exclaimed, "It went great! They got more done than they thought they would, and we finished an hour early."

I said, "That's tremendous." Then melancholy fell over her, and I said, "Well, then, what's wrong?" She said, "They think they did it themselves!"

Somewhere in her response I began to sense she had stumbled on to a profound secret about facilitation. We stand for something as facilitators. Now the trick is to stand for something so transparently that you do not disrupt their own process. How do you become the invisible rock in the middle of the table that will be the point around which the group can have guidance?

Facilitators are best
When people barely know they exist.
Their work done, their aim fulfilled,
People will say,
"We did it ourselves."
  — Adapted from Lao Tzu

I have heard people ask, "Now why do these workshops have to be led? Why can't we all sit around the table and shoot the breeze on the topic and come to a conclusion?" Doesn't the attempt to 'lead' destroy spontaneity and take all the fun out of it, especially if the process is predictable?"

Wow! Well, maybe. If no one attempted to grandstand, argue, play dumb, or pontificate at length. But experience has shown that if someone takes time to think through the workshop, to reflect on the group and where it has been, and stage-manage the process to a conclusion, things flow much better towards a great product.

LAUNCHING A CONSENSUS WORKSHOP

The first thing to decide is whether to use the cards method or the flip chart approach. How many pieces of data do you want? How many people do you have in the group? If the group is larger and you want more than 20 pieces of data, use cards. For a smaller group producing less data, the flip chart approach is better.

Go through the design and preparation steps laid out in Chapter 10. Pay special attention to isolating your focus question. Then consider the following:

1. Make the setting suitable
Although some workshops have been done in the open with the flip chart attached to a big tree, normally you need a room that fits the size of the group. It helps group dynamics if the room is neither too small nor too big. Check the room to see whether there's a blackboard, easel, or suitable wall. For a major consensus workshop with many people, you will need a large wall space. (See Chapter 13 on wall spaces.) It's good to check with the sponsor to see if they object to your sticking cards on the wall for an hour or so.

The wall will largely determine the alignment of the tables. There should be enough surrounding space to allow participants to move in and out easily during breaks, but still allow all participants to see the data on the wall. A table for refreshments at the back or side of the room helps keep people anchored in the room. Ensure you have adequate time allotted for the event, so that you don't have to rush the process.

2. Invite participants to take their places

Invite the group to come in and sit down. Have only as many chairs as there are people. Take up a position at the head of the table. Make sure you have markers, cards, and tape or putty with you.

It is elementary to stand at the front of the room, but symbolically important. It says that you intend to take charge of the proceedings. Putting the flip chart in the middle says that you intend it to be seen. It is a primary tool.

Once, I attended an education day at a hospital. When I entered the room, I saw that it was beautifully set up, with tables and chairs in a U shape, easel and tablet at the front, snacks at the side of the room, washrooms close by — an ideal room for a workshop. However, the teacher, before beginning, picked up the easel and plunked it down on the left front side of the room and did her instruction from there. Why, why, why? I kept asking myself, completely distracted. As a consequence, everyone on the left side of the room had to twist their necks to the left, and attempt to write notes at the same time.

Later I decided that this facilitator had selfhood problems. She had not decided 100 per cent to be the facilitator — to be an up-front person facing the group without apology. She had to be off to the side. A pity.

3. Get started

Start with some opening remarks. If the group is talking, wait for a natural break in the conversation to begin. Most often participants come to order if you wait for a break in the conversation, and say something like, "Well, let's get started." You may want to start with an icebreaker — a short conversation that introduces the participants to each other or a quick conversation on something they did on the weekend. Icebreakers need to be short. When there is a tough workshop coming up, participants may want to try a few ruses to postpone it.

4. Do the method

Proceed with the method. Give the context, write the focus question on the board, rehearse the working assumptions, get the brainstorm up, cluster the data, name the clusters, and do the reflective conversation (see Chapters 3 to 9).

FACILITATOR COMPETENCIES

The style question is how to combine a great up-front presence with expert technique. Charisma without expertise provides great drama but possibly no product. An infallibly applied technique without a beckoning style may provide an impeccable product, but a session without passion or joy. The challenge is to combine both art and science in the act of facilitation. The workshop facilitator's style and attitude are key factors in establishing a participatory environment.

Facilitators who assume the group can work together in a positive and creative way will find ways for that to happen. If they emphasize difficulties, this will amplify problems. The facilitator elicits input, raises questions that help the group cluster and relate ideas. A balance of high play and an earnest search for meaning is the style most helpful. People name the patterns they see, and reality takes on a new cast. The group generates new knowledge, creates significance and a common understanding of their world. Together they create a new constellation of reality.

In this context, the workshop facilitator's style might be best summed up as a set of competencies that the consensus workshop facilitator can display.

Competency 1: The facilitator uses the method effectively

The facilitator is competent in designing and leading larger or smaller group processes. This requires a familiarity with the process of creating and sequencing questions that move the group from surface considerations into the depth implications of any topic. Underneath this is the capacity to distinguish process from content, and the discernment to decide what the group needs at any point.

Competency 2: The facilitator uses time and space intentionally

It is not enough to merely select a good space for the workshop. The facilitator has to know how to create the environment for the event. If the janitor has not cleaned the space, the facilitator has to do it, and, at break times, keep things orderly to ensure that the environment remains an ally of the event. It is important to know how to best arrange the space so that it works for both the process and the group. This means checking out the space ahead of time and making sure there are walls appropriate for holding data. It means arranging the tables and chairs to communicate intentionality and maximize face-to-face participation. It also means skillfully using decor tuned to the nature of the event. The facilitator also has to be a kind of metronome for the group, sensing the rhythm that is most enlivening at a particular time of day; pacing the activities so as to capitalize on the "beat" of the group; apportioning available time both to get the job done and to reach timely closure. (See Chapter 13: Time, Space, Mood and Group.)

Competency 3: The facilitator is skillful in evoking participation and creativity

More than knowledge of methods, the facilitator also has to be a group evocateur, with an unshakable belief that the group itself has the wisdom and creativity needed to deal with the situation. What is involved here is the ability to create a climate of participation. The facilitator knows how to·elicit the latent wisdom of the group, catalyse everyone's participation, and involve the whole group in taking responsibility for its decisions. The ability to create a group climate conducive to both participation and creativity involves a variety of ways of relating to different sorts of people. Eliciting participants' wisdom is the name of the game. It is here that the facilitator needs sensitivity and adroitness. The adroit facilitator must set a context to help the participants focus their insights in response to a focus question.

Competency 4: The facilitator honors the group and affirms its wisdom

Appropriating a group's diversity as a gift is more than just a skill. It involves much more than a facile "I'm OK — you're OK" attitude. Honoring the group requires the ability to recognize the wonder of life and the essential greatness of each human being. It involves a constant decision to interpret situations positively, and the habit of responding with a "yes" before a "no." The facilitator is aware that the method works best when affirming the wisdom of each individual person, honoring the collective data of the whole group, and celebrating its completed work. This is not just an abstract principle. In practice it entails the ability and readiness to listen carefully to participants' words, to accept silence with understanding, to maintain accepting eye contact with each speaker, and to note down individual insights verbatim. It also means being willing to focus on what group members are saying rather than what you are going to say next. The other side of honoring a participant is the readiness to push confusing answers for clarity to reveal the real insight.

Competency 5: The facilitator is capable of maintaining objectivity

A key role of the facilitator is to provide objectivity to the group process. While one side of the facilitator is more like an orchestra conductor who wants first-class music, the other side is more like a dispassionate referee who knows the importance of maintaining a neutral stance toward the game. The facilitator sets aside personal opinions about the group's ideas, being careful not to react negatively to its insights. This same neutral stance requires the capacity to handle criticism, anger and frustration non-defensively, whenever the group energy overheats.

Competency 6: The facilitator is skilled in 'reading' the underlying dynamics in the group

The facilitator is practiced in sensing dynamics in the group. In particular, facilitators pay particular attention to interpreting the silence of the group, whether it comes from confusion, fear, anger, or shyness. This extends to sensing the group's uncertainty at particular points and taking steps to help them move through it. A facilitator must quickly identify hidden agendas by picking up non-verbal cues. The facilitator listens, as it were, with a third ear, to pick up the significance of what lies behind participants' words. On the more active side, the facilitator is able to push negatively-phrased data for its underlying insight and to probe vague answers for their fuller meaning.

Competency 7: The facilitator orchestrates the event drama

Paramount to engaging the group's commitment to the workshop process is the development of audience rapport. The facilitator engages this rapport from the start, creating social icebreakers that loosen up the group at the beginning of a workshop. Then, as participants go through their alternating ups and downs, the facilitator is inventive in shifting the pace and mood to get the job done, and using personal illustrations to release the group. Experience brings a capacity to use humor in a helpful way. Practice brings the sensitivity to know when the group needs a break or when the pace of work needs changing. A facilitator especially needs sensitivity to the critical points where something really important must be handled before moving on. The facilitator needs to sense whether the group is ready to push for a breakthrough on a difficult issue.

Competency 8: The facilitator releases blocks to the process

The facilitator has to learn how to use a light touch to gently discourage side conversations, as well as shrewd tactics to dissuade speechifying and argumentation. Tact is sometimes needed to discourage the dominance of particular individuals, handle "difficult" behaviors, and deal helpfully with conflict. If need be, the facilitator should be ready to apologize and take blame for difficulties, so the group can move on. In thorny situations, the facilitator has to be able to bring the decision of how to proceed back to the group, so that it can take responsibility for its own process.

Competency 9: The facilitator is nimble in adapting to the changing situation

Facilitation is like a balancing act on the high wire, requiring the capacity to flex with a changing situation. The facilitator knows how to balance the process on the one hand, and the results of the process on the other, to harmonize the needs of the participants at any one moment with the demands of the process. The root of this skill is the understanding that the process for arriving at the results is just as important as the results themselves. A certain mental nimbleness is mandatory so that when the unexpected happens, the facilitator can think and make decisions on the fly and use the methods flexibly.

Competency 10: The facilitator can produce powerful documentation
Coming up with a useful group product — a documentary record of the group's insights — is the bottom line of facilitation. With the help of an assigned documenter who types up the group data and decisions during the process, the participants can be handed a hard-copy product before they leave. The documenter has to keep track of all the data generated by the group and use the available software, typewriters or copiers to produce the final tables and documents.

THE FUNDAMENTAL REQUIREMENT

These competencies are not "oughts." Facilitation simply won't work — people will get angry or stop participating honestly — unless at least the following two conditions are in place.
1. The group trusts that while you are facilitating you are detached from your own opinions. Notice this doesn't say you don't have any opinions: It means they trust that you have let go of them and are listening without bias while you are up front.
2. You trust that while you are facilitating you are detached from your opinions. If you are secretly manipulating the group towards your own answers, it will show in your work, and the group will stop trusting you.

One facilitator repeats a mantra to herself over and over to maintain this: Her mantra is: "I am curious." This is shorthand for the question she asks herself before starting a workshop: "What new things can I learn from this group's insight and how they get to it?" This jogs her memory to set aside her own opinions while she is facilitating.

THE PARADOX OF FACILITATORS

Many of the qualities needed by consensus workshop facilitators fall into pairs of opposites that are in tension with each other. F. Scott Fitzgerald said that the test of intelligence is the ability to hold two opposed ideas in mind at the same time and still retain the ability to function. These are some of the opposed ideas the facilitator has to hold in his mind and operate from:

Encourages participation	←——→	Discourages individual dominance
Nonchalant	←——→	Alert
Goes for a product	←——→	Pays attention to detail
Honors the group	←——→	Honors the individuals
Takes given data	←——→	Pushes for depth
Elucidates through questions	←——→	Elucidates through context
Holds to the timeline	←——→	Lets the group take time to struggle
Keeps process moving	←——→	Deals with difficulties in the group
Expert technique	←——→	Stylistic flair
Loyal to the method	←——→	Group evocateur
Flexibility	←——→	On track

FACILITATION BY THE BOSS OR THE EXPERT

It is difficult, but not impossible, for bosses or experts to be facilitators. If they decide to facilitate, they need to be crystal-clear about a few things:

- To avoid conflict of interest, they need to be very clear on which role — expert or facilitator — they are playing, and make sure that others know they have decided to play that role.
- As facilitators they need to keep to the process and not shift into other roles. If they feel they absolutely have to shift roles momentarily to that of expert, they need to tell participants they are taking off their facilitator hat to play the role of expert for a little while. When finished that, they must tell the group they are now putting on the hat of facilitator again.
- They need to be committed to people's participation and the value of participants' ideas.
- They need to know when they can present their own ideas and when they can't. If they want to be in the workshop as participants, they need to shift to the side of the table.

BE THE ONE YOU ARE

Once a trainee under the mentorship of Jo Nelson approached her after a style workshop and said: "You know, Jo, all this is well and good about competencies, and changing styles like a chameleon, but I am who I am and I'm not up to all these personal pyrotechnics. I'm a very simple straightforward person, and I can't help that."

Jo replied to that in three short sentences: "Fine, just be that simple, straightforward person to the hilt as you do the workshop and it will be enough. All the other traits you have a lifetime to develop. It's only the next step of competency that is required of you now."

CHALLENGES THAT STRETCH THE FACILITATOR

> The difference between a warrior and an ordinary man is that a warrior sees
> everything as a challenge, while an ordinary man sees everything as either a
> blessing or a curse.
> Carlos Casteneda

DIFFICULT PEOPLE OR DIFFICULT BEHAVIORS

The workshop leader may have a superb plan for a workshop, but it does not always go
as planned. Situations come up which have to be dealt with on the spot. People often ask,
"How do you deal with 'difficult' participants? At times, people's behavior can tax a
workshop leader's skills and patience to the limit.

Wayne Nelson tells this story:

At a facilitator's conference, a woman asked me, "How do you deal with difficult participants?"
Knowing I was avoiding the question, I gave my standard reply: "There are no difficult participants.
The ToP™ methods treat every person as inherently valuable with real wisdom to contribute."

"But surely," she pushed, "surely you have encountered people who have sorely tried your patience,
and made you stretch a great deal?"

"Yes," I said, "I have to admit that the behavior of some people puts one on a rack, where you either
stretch enough or you break. But this is the true test of the facilitator's art."

So, there are no "difficult" participants, only difficult behaviors — no, only behaviors that stretch the facilitator's leadership. That may seem like splitting hairs, but these days we all understand how our images affect our behavior. If workshop leaders, either before or during a workshop, build up in their minds the image that certain participants or behaviors are "difficult," they will consciously or unconsciously begin to treat those participants differently, and tend to discount their contributions. Those persons will not be heard, listened to, or affirmed as inherently valuable with real wisdom to contribute.

We all need to be reminded that, on the whole, facilitation is less focused on dealing with "difficult" behavior than it is on enabling each person to think, act, and be at their best. The facilitator emphasizes the positive rather than reacts to the negative. At the same time, we need to recognize that many of the difficult or objectionable behaviors in groups have their roots in an environment in which participation is restricted. If the facilitator's role is focused on behavioral control, behavior can be expected to surface. Much difficult behavior stems from bad process in which people are not heard, listened to, or affirmed.

The environment that people are in often affects how they participate — their willingness to listen, their expectation of being heard, and their tendency to argue. By bringing in an effective process, like the workshop, with its inherent respect for individuals and its basis of synthesizing ideas rather than combating or analysing them, you, as a facilitator, are dramatically shifting the environment. Participants then will respond differently to the situation and many expected problems will disappear.

So, what do these "difficult behaviors" — the ones that stretch the facilitator's expertise — look like in a workshop?

1. Commandeering the workshop

What happens when an academic commandeers a workshop with his lecture, attacking what participants have said and implying that other participants are not qualified to deal with the topic? One facilitator tells this story:

> Some time ago, I facilitated a two-part consultation with health professionals, where the second session built on the first. The second day had new participants, so I started with a conversation to reflect on the opening session so as to bring the new people up to speed. One of the participants, a well-respected and knowledgeable academic, tried to commandeer the reflective discussion. What was intended as a brief review turned into a painfully long series of verbal essays from the professor. He attacked things people

had said in the previous session. He implied that other participants were not qualified to deal with the topic. He intimated that he knew best.

We heard him out, then belatedly began the second session. It was interesting that, once I started the brainstorming workshop using cards, he seemed to melt into the group so that everyone was participating with animation, when just moments before they were edgy and detached. The card-storming process enabled the professor to focus, and the quieter community representatives to get their ideas in.

There are indirect ways to counteract this commandeering behavior. When beginning a session, you can point out that everyone's thoughts are valuable and everyone's insight is needed for the best results. After a context and the focus question, give the participants time to write down their own answers before they speak. Give an example of the kind of response that is on target.

On the first question, it helps to get one response from each person. This tends to break the ice for everyone and make subsequent participation easier. Then open the discussion to the whole group. Make a point to acknowledge participants' ideas respectfully, because this encourages everyone to participate.

One facilitator deals with this behavior more directly. He listens to the academic attentively, then, as soon as the professor stops to draw breath, the facilitator says, "This is what I heard you saying," and summarizes the speech in a few points, then says, "Someone else?" The trick is to wait for the opportunity and be very fast off the mark. Make sure the academic's main points are included in the brainstorm. Before placing a card in a cluster, always get more than one nod — usually get several — from different parts of the room. This ensures that no one person alone can manipulate the results.

2. The bully

It seems a truism that the first level of participation is about getting ideas out and enabling people to actually hear each other. If someone in the group decides to vent built-up frustration, you can simply write the comment down. The participant will probably be quite surprised. Some people are used to being treated as outsiders, as enemies, or as people who don't matter.

One facilitator, preparing for a strategic planning retreat with a group of public-sector managers, received a warning about one of the group leaders, Monica. Apparently

Monica had a reputation for being strident, pushy and argumentative. As the facilitator prepared the workshop, she wondered how on earth she was going to deal with Monica. In starting the session, the workshop leader made a point of emphasizing the importance of respect for each person's input. She talked about active listening and made sure each participant contributed to the discussion. After three sessions, she realized that no one was displaying the behaviors she had been warned about. She checked that the person in question was still in the room, and was assured that she was.

Because the whole discussion was conducted with respect, Monica's ideas were heard, the workshops were creative and productive and the potentially destructive behavior never surfaced. Monica's facial mannerisms had softened, and she contributed creatively and helpfully.

3. Participating not wisely, but too well

Members of a group may over-participate. Their creativity begins to bubble over, their ideas pour forth, so that others' participation is hindered. An indirect approach is useful here. If a few people seem to be carrying most of the conversation, simply ask to hear from others. Ask for responses from the other side of the room, or from those who have not yet spoken. That usually gets the message across. Gentle teasing in situations like this requires a lot of sensivity but it can allow highly vocal people to see their own behavior, and may give the group permission to even out the participation in its own way. Calling directly on silent participants is risky, but, done gently and with respect, it can help people find their voice.

4. The quiet ones

Facilitation writer Sam Kaner reflects on the phenomenon of quiet people in a group:

> People refrain from saying what they're really thinking for a wide variety of reasons. Sometimes they hold back because the risk is too great. But people also keep quiet because they aren't sure whether their ideas are worth saying, or because they can't turn the kernels of their ideas into fully formed contributions. There are many occasions when participants, if they were given a little support, permission or a nudge, might go ahead and say what's on their mind. Yet without that support, they often stay quiet.

Many people tend to be quiet in large groups, but smaller teams focused on specific questions may help to engage the quiet ones and make it harder for a few vocal people to dominate the discussion. Each small team needs a specific assignment, a set of procedures and a reminder to ask the first question of each member of the group in turn.

People participate and learn in different ways. Affirming diverse styles and using non-verbal techniques (such as drawings, diagrams, stories or drama) helps people participate in ways that emphasize their strengths. Using several modes of thinking and interaction balances participation more effectively than dealing directly with quiet individuals.

When certain people can't understand what others are saying, they tune out. In that case, it's always appropriate to suggest that participants ask the speakers to clarify their words. Sometimes just saying things in a slightly different way is enough. It takes very little time to restate or explain an idea; just ask for a phrase or a sentence.

Toronto facilitator John Miller comments on how each stage of this workshop method evokes different learning capacities:

> It is apparent to me that different steps of the process engage different kinds of thinking, so some people can participate in the stages of the workshop according to their thinking preferences. With this in mind, the facilitator can trust the process and accept varying levels of participation from each member of the group.

For example, I have met people who cannot brainstorm, but get actively involved in naming the clusters. I've seen some people who were most acutely engaged in seeing connections among cards, helping their colleagues form clusters of ideas. I've even seen people who can barely tolerate the whole process who came to life at the end when it became evident that decisions had gelled and everyone was committed.

5. The flamethrower

You may run across participants who speak in a vexatious, somewhat inflammatory, manner. In this case, you need to keep asking them to restate their response so it more directly answers the question. The participant will probably get the point and tone down the rhetoric. It may take some effort, but, if done respectfully, it should work. Sometimes a facilitator can respectfully reframe a participant's words to capture the essence of their meaning, while deleting the heavy energy that prevents other participants from hearing their insight. Starting from the assumption that this person has a piece of the puzzle allows the facilitator to do this with respect.

Occasionally, someone in the group will make a cheap shot — a witty or snide remark that insults someone. A cheap shot generally makes the target feel bad and does not help the group. Roger Schwartz points out that those who have been the objects of a cheap shot spend time thinking about the comment, or thinking up clever comebacks to use later on. In the process, the person is distracted. The result may be a withholding of consent later on. On very rare occasions, the workshop may be coming to a close in fine fashion, and suddenly you may hear, "Well, I, for one, have no intention of implementing this decision, or even agreeing with the workshop." Here, you could ask what part of the results they disagree with, or what is the issue. Get out the detail so the group can respond to something concrete. It may be necessary to give a short context, referring back to the working assumptions, such as "There are no wrong answers," or "We need everyone's wisdom."

6. When things get hot

Suppose you are moving along in a session and an argument breaks out. What do you do? There are certain understandings to build on.
- Tension is a sign that a group is healthy and thinking.
- A diversity of views is valuable to ensure that decisions are sound and well through-through.
- Groups do need to gain an understanding of the perspectives involved, resolve issues, and make choices.
- Most arguments happen when people are really getting to the central questions and are moving toward choices.

The key is to keep the dialogue clearly related to the original focus question and to allow ideas to stand independently rather than in opposition. Sometimes when Mary Smith's independent idea comes after Ben Jones' independent idea, Ben assumes that her idea is intended to contradict his, rather than simply be a different idea. Ben unnecessarily blows his top.

In this case, refer the group back to the original question and ask people to clearly state their points of view one at a time, so the varying perspectives are standing side by side. It's helpful to have the group examine the assumptions inherent in the various points of view.

Ask each participant, "Why do you think this?" Then they can think together and make the necessary choices. This way helps a group to deal with complexity and form a common mind. Shifting out of a debating mode into consensus building makes all the difference in the world. People want their ideas to count, and the consensus workshop lets that happen without pushing or competition.

If an argument gets hot, sometimes a facilitator has to step in, break the flow, and structure it. Using the four levels of the focused conversation method, create a set of questions on the spot that focus the conversation. This gives participants a way to step back, reflect, and hear the relevant experiences which lie behind each other's feelings and convictions. When the conversation has progressed to an appropriate point, ask someone who is more detached to state what they believe to be the consensus. In these situations, it is important that the discussion be respectful and focused on the central question, and doesn't spill over into judgmental statements about individuals. You may need to say this directly to the group.

If the conversation becomes very heated, or so tangled that resolution seems impossible, a break can help. Before people stand up, leave them with a question to move them forward. When they return, recap the major points made previously and follow the conversation through to its most reasonable conclusion. Sometimes a separate conversation or another session is needed. Another option is to form a small task force to consider the matter and bring a recommendation back to the group. The report and conversation usually lead to a resolution or statement of consensus.

7. The gangbuster

At the beginning of one public consultation, a woman stood up and wanted to present a prepared analysis and proposal statement. The leader told her the meeting process would use everyone's insights, but she demanded that the group deal with her statement immediately. It was a tense and rocky moment. It became clear that she was not alone. Many others in the room had given this concern a lot of thought and needed to be heard. It took time to listen, empathize, and allow her to see that others also had concerns, but she reluctantly stepped back and participated with the rest of the group in what could have been a hijacked situation.

People are concerned about the quality of participation and getting helpful results. If they fear that things will not go well, they may raise questions about the process. Take the time to answer questions; authentic questions deserve real answers. But if process becomes the primary focus, you will lose time and energy. If things are moving along, such questions can be deferred by asking the person to write down the question. I try to deal with these questions at a time when I can focus on them more helpfully. The facilitator can give choices to the group, present the group with alternatives and their consequences, and let the group choose or create another alternative. This can be time-consuming, but the group will trust the process that is chosen.

Sometimes it can seem as though the universe is conspiring to give the facilitator a really hard time. The client is dissatisfied and demanding, the group is bad-tempered and argumentative, the space is cramped and uncomfortable, and the snacks are served at the wrong time. It is only too easy to start asking, "Why me? I'm such a good facilitator." But, as someone said, "Expecting the world to treat you fairly because you are good is like expecting the bull not to charge because you are a vegetarian."

It is good for the facilitator to remember stories like *The Man in the Bowler Hat*, originally a four-minute movie. The story features a little man in a bowler hat who is walking down a lane.

He comes to a brick wall. He goes to the side and sits down. A few minutes later, another little man in a bowler hat comes down the lane. Seeing the brick wall, he backs up and runs with all his strength and butts the wall down with his head. He lies there in the debris. The first little man gets up, walks through the hole in the wall and over the other man, and continues down the lane. Suddenly he comes to another wall! Once again, he goes to the side and sits down. The second little man in the bowler hat, somewhat re-invigorated by now, sees the brick wall, backs up, then runs with all his strength and butts down the second wall. The man waiting by the side walks through.

The capacity to keep on dealing with whatever challenges come up is the kind of iron needed in the facilitator's being — to keep butting down every wall standing in the way of the group, so that it may pass through and claim its future.

8. Taking on the facilitator

Occasionally a participant will take on the facilitator, questioning qualifications, or the meeting process itself. What to do? The ability to separate self from process, and process from results, provides a key to success. The ultimate question is, "What needs to happen so that this group gets the results it needs?" A group cannot get results from a process that it will not use. You can try to persuade the group to go your way, suggest an alternative, or create a discussion that will help the group to create its own model. People need to examine the options and consequences carefully; be sure to point out that the time available begins after this discussion. These events are hard on the facilitator and the group, but they can also be extremely creative as learning experiences, so try to go gently and tread lightly. A facilitator needs patience, flexibility and faith in the group's capacity to work its way through issues.

9. The unpredictable

Sometimes, unpredictable things happen, as in this story told by Jo Nelson:

> North of Yellowknife by the side of a lake, accessible only by floatplane, I was doing a workshop in a tiny room with forty Dene. The Dene are caribou hunters. At one point the room got very warm. I decided it would be helpful if we all went outside for a while, so we took the portable white board with us to continue the workshop in some fresh air. When rain came we sat on picnic tables with tarps rigged over our heads and wrote and grouped the cards.
>
> At one point a herd of caribou appeared by the lake. The will of the group was very obvious. They looked at me. I gave a nod, and half the group picked up their rifles and went to hunt caribou, with the promise that they would do the naming when they got back. The rest of the group was adamant: "Well, we can't leave the clusters hanging like this. We must name them." So they did the titles. When the rest of the group returned with caribou, they were shown the holding titles. They accepted the representational work of the others in the group. And everyone welcomed the caribou feast that night.

This was probably the only time in consensus workshop history when participants walked into the room with briefcases and high-powered rifles. Incidents like this that completely upset the apple cart remind the facilitator that the participants really do own the workshop.

USING THE METHOD TO DEAL WITH THE ISSUES

The reader may notice that in each of the examples above, no extraordinary measures were used to counteract unhelpful behavior. No one was taken out of the room and read the riot act; there were no pitched battles between facilitator and participant. At no point does the facilitator turn into a behavior counsellor. The only things used to deal with the behavior are various aspects of the method, such as:

- Summarizing a long speech and including its main points in the brainstorm
- Emphasizing respect for participants' ideas
- Asking for responses from around the table
- Asking another question
- Referring back to the focus question
- Taking a break
- Encouraging questions for clarity
- Rehearsing the context.

A workshop is not the place for interventions of behavioral psychology or participant counselling. When all participants get the respect they deserve, strange behaviors become rare.

We need to remember that we are turning the tables as we open the dialogue and structure authentic participation. When we receive and honor every response, we thumb our noses at those who claim that higher authority or exclusive knowledge should override the collective wisdom of everyone concerned. Building consensus forms a common will and in doing so, enables a shift into a new style.

A beginner might say after reading this chapter, "Golly, you're asking a heck of a lot from people!" True, but on the marathon journey of becoming a great workshop facilitator, it's only the next few yards in proficiency that is required, not the whole 26 miles. When *New York Daily News* cartoonist Bill Gatto was asked how long it took him to draw a cartoon, he replied, "Two hours and 40 years." An old-time facilitator, asked how long it takes to do a great consensus workshop, might say the same thing.

13

TIME, SPACE, MOOD AND GROUP

All you have to do to change an unhappy or dissatisfying situation is
to answer the question, "How do I want this situation to become?"
Then you commit totally to actions that carry you there.
Azie Taylor Morton

THE MAJOR KEY to success in leading workshops is doing the method competently
and with style. However, there are other keys. Underneath the components mentioned
below are the primary values of:
   • what it takes to get the job done
   • what is communicated to the group indirectly
   • holding the tension between honoring the process and honoring the group.

MANAGING TIME EFFECTIVELY

Managing time effectively has to do with workshop scheduling, arriving early, beginning
at the right time, pacing the process, and finishing on time.

1. Schedule events carefully

Events need to be scheduled with participants in mind, which means scheduling
workshop events when the participants can come. The leader needs to know the yearly
rhythm of the group and avoid times dedicated to other things. For some groups,
scheduling the appropriate time of day is critical. Most groups will not yield many bright

ideas after three o'clock in the afternoon, or just before a looming work deadline. It is important to consult with the participants to find the right date and time of day.

It is also important to schedule enough time to do justice to the topic. Some groups make the mistake of not allowing enough time for difficult decisions to be made. A workshop on a simple topic may take 30 minutes. One that needs thoughtful, serious dialogue may take three to four hours. Most workshops need at least one to two hours for effective results.

2. Arrive early

Effective workshop leaders honor the group by being on-site early enough to be totally prepared. Everything should be ready when people begin to arrive. This punctuality enables effective preparation and attention to all of the details. An early facilitator is there to welcome participants and set an atmosphere of colleagues tackling a task. Being on time communicates seriousness.

Facilitators have been known to come into the workshop room late, huffing and puffing, saying how busy they've been. That is communicating "me-me," rather than focusing on the participants' needs. Workshop facilitators need to get everything personal out of the way so they can focus on the participants.

3. Begin at an appropriate time

Every group has its own culture. While time is planned very carefully, a workshop plan must be balanced with the group's norms and expectations. So, starting precisely on time with few participants may communicate more respect for them than the rest of the participants. However, allowing too much time beyond the declared starting time does not honor those who made the effort to be on time. It's often helpful to discuss starting time with those who are present. The group can select a time to begin and plan to involve those who come later.

4. Pace the process

Pacing is the key to effective facilitation. Pacing is related to the time of the day, as well as to the requirements of the process. The workshop leader is always aware of the time. As in running a distance race, a leader needs to know when to move quickly and when to slow down. Constant monitoring of time is necessary. Some facilitators place their watch on the table or use a small clock. If the facilitator is seated, the pace will often slow down and become more reflective. Moving too fast may indicate a lack of resolution.

Varying the pace can keep the event interesting, and moving around the room will pick up the pace. A slow pace is helpful for careful, deliberate conversation. A quick pace can encourage the use of intuition. Following the same slow, plodding rhythm throughout is likely to put participants to sleep.

5. Finish on time

A workshop leader may need to wait to begin a session, but it is almost always necessary to finish at the agreed time. Participants often make commitments based on your scheduled ending time, and running overtime violates people's commitment. If extra time is required, it should be discussed with the group: "Do I have your permission to go for another ten minutes?" If substantial additional time is required, consider scheduling another session. It is good to check with the group at the beginning of the workshop to learn who will be inconvenienced if the workshop goes overtime. There may be people with planes to catch, or those with particular medical conditions.

MANAGING SPACE

As a leader, you must order the workshop space so that it is aesthetically pleasing and practically helpful. In a well-prepared space, tables and chairs are in alignment. The space also has appropriate wall space and decor. In a well-prepared room, the space should communicate, "We mean business: What is going on here is important."

Getting the space working for you

For a workshop you will need enough tables and chairs for the participants, but not too many, and a flip chart with an easel to hold it. Always check to see whether the materials you need will be on-site. There should be enough space surrounding the tables to allow participants to move in and out easily during breaks. A table with snacks and refreshments at the back of the room helps groups stay anchored in the room during longer workshops.

The environment of the workshop always communicates a message. There are some spaces that are so bad that not even the greatest workshop leader in the world could pull anything off. Having said that, a determined facilitator can make the best of whatever space. Wayne Nelson tells of a time in Uganda when he was to facilitate a community development group of 60 people on the edge of Kampala. He was shown to a community hall with a stage, no door and a dirt floor. They cleaned it out and were able to have a great workshop.

Walls

Selecting the wall for placing data can be difficult. You need a flat blank vertical wall at least eight feet by eight feet. If the front wall has a black or white board attached, you need to figure out how you will deal with that, or switch to a side wall, and orient the seating differently.

Good and Bad Walls

BEST WALLS	WORST WALLS
Semi-gloss smooth walls	Brick walls
	Corduroy walls
	Walls with décor moldings
	Walls with peeling paint

Some situations really test the workshop leader's creativity. One workshop leader finished up attaching the group's ideas to a chandelier. Another facilitator had to do a workshop in an old house dating from the late 19th century. The walls were covered in silk, so he couldn't hang anything from them. He attached the group's ideas to the doors, then transferred them to tape loops hanging from the fireplace. Another facilitator, doing a workshop in the far north of Canada, had to attach cards to the side of a teepee. Another workshop in a village in India attached the flip chart sheet to a baobab tree; printing was a real trick. If you have walls that are difficult, a repositionable spray adhesive can be very useful in providing a clean surface. Whatever the space, you have to get the ideas up in front of the group, attached to whatever is there.

It is good to check with the building managers to get permission to attach things to the wall. Most people seem to use either putty or masking tape to attach the cards or paper. Great care needs to be taken when removing these from the wall after the workshop (Yes, you do need to remove them!), as the paint needs to stay intact. One beginning workshop leader got the bright idea of using duct tape. The owner insisted on a repaint at the leader's expense.

Centerpiece table

We recommend that facilitators use a "centerpiece" at the center of the meeting space. A centerpiece is a central table or place in the center of the table, which is set with some tasteful objects of art or symbolism.

Items placed on the centerpiece table need to be symbolic, not pretty. Examples of appropriate items on the table are a cloth, a company symbol or mission statement, a

SET-UP	ADVANTAGE	DISADVANTAGE
Four tables squared off with centerpiece table	• Everyone visible • Clear view of wall • Room for centerpiece • Ordered, intentional • Teamwork easy	• If there are more than 30 people, many people are too far from the front wall.
Squared off tables for a small group	• Tight arrangement for a group of 20	• People can't see each other very well. • Difficulty in moving around
Echelon format	• Good for large groups • Ease of movement	• Writing cards is difficult • People are looking at the backs of each others' heads
Round tables in semi-circle with décor table in middle	• Works well for really large groups.	• Leaves a big open space in the middle

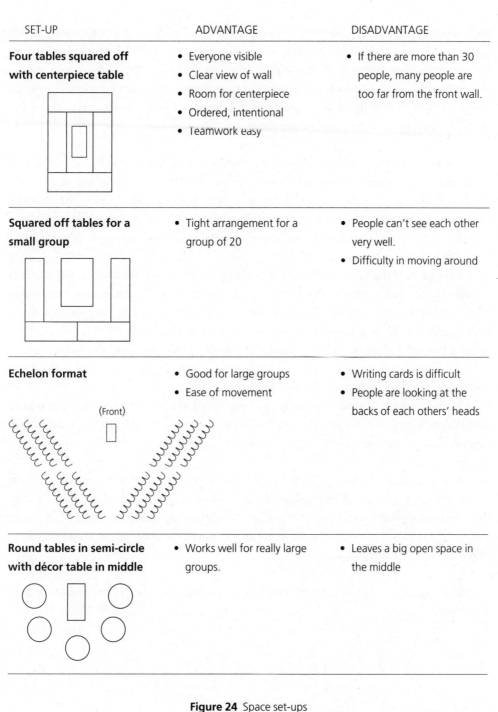

Figure 24 Space set-ups

rock, a plant, pebbles, an aboriginal artform, or flowers. Nothing too fancy; use quotes, pictures or icons that hold the task of the group. An architects' group might have cardboard buildings or models. A teachers' group might have books. The objects should not be high enough to block the group's line of vision. Candles or incense suggest a religious purpose for the workshop. Keep it simple and elegant; don't try to put the whole kitchen sink on the table. Less is more.

A centerpiece can focus the group's attention when it wanders, and can provide a pleasant environmental stimulus in a bare or cluttered room. An appropriate centerpiece in the middle of the tables ties the group together and reminds everyone that the decision-making power is in the center of the table. It also gives participants a place to rest their eyes and, in an indirect way, brings participants back to the topic. (Figure 24)

The centerpiece in the middle of the group is the mediating power of the workshop. It stands for the objective reality, namely the mission or task that mediates the participants' relationship to each other. It reminds participants that they are not in this workshop because they get on well together or because they are soul mates, or because they think alike. They are there because they have a common job to do, a problem to solve, a plan to create, a decision to make.

Décor

The workshop leader inspects the room an hour ahead of time, rearranging the furniture and décor. The aim is to provide a milieu that announces to the participants as they arrive: "Something momentous is going to happen here."

For longer sessions, the unused walls can hold some decor items that are in sync with the event, such as a diagram of the process. Decor placed at eye level has maximum impact. If some of the room's standard decor is likely to distract the group or suggest a different task entirely, you might consider taking it down for the duration of the session, making sure you replace it afterwards.

Time and space are the objective dimensions of facilitation. They either help or hinder the process.

MANAGING THE MOOD: CREATING EVENTFULNESS

Effective workshops are interesting, engaging, and exciting. Ineffective workshops are deadening, boring, and often unproductive. The content of the workshop is always the important thing, and ensuring high-quality content is always the leader's first responsibility.

In addition, techniques can be used to nurture involvement in the group and hold boredom at bay. Here are six ways to keep a group engaged.

1. Balance types of activities

Variety is the spice of life. Use a spectrum of activities to keep the group interested and engaged — discussions, individual reflection, pair exercises, small group work, and whole-group plenary discussions. This enables people with different learning styles and comfort levels to participate. Jeanette Stanfield tells of her experience in an ICA strategy consultation:

> I walked into the meeting room and was surprised to see brightly colored slinkies, cards, yo-yos and some other colorful, textured, mysterious "stuff" on the ordered tables. The kinesthetically minded among us had a ball playing with these objects. The visual people delighted in the colour and design. The auditory learners quickly moved from words to images. The more intellectual among us were somewhat offended.
>
> The upshot was a workshop where all kinds of wisdom came out of the woodwork that I had rarely seen before in this group, including experiences of healing among the members. The facilitator just went ahead and asked her questions and let the environment do its work.

In many business environments, people may not have permission to share the subjective, intuitive, wild wisdom they possess. Coffee-break times, complaint boxes or lunch rooms may be the only places where creative interplay seems permitted. Highly creative solutions can arise when participants are encouraged to use the right hemisphere of their brains. When rational and intuitive insights are integrated, the clustering step is enriched. When people are given permission to use their more intuitive side, unnoticed employees may find they have the keys to the organization's future.

2. Keep people moving

You want to catalyse some real creativity in your participants' responses. So you have to find ways to stimulate fresh attention and imagination. Nothing is so deadening as sitting in the same seat for hours on end. New faces and perspectives challenge participants and enhance the dialogue. What can be done? Mix people up so they interact with different people, especially when they don't know each other very well.

Move between team and plenary groups. Time your activities so people have natural opportunities to move. Schedule breaks where appropriate, and do some stretching and breathing exercises to keep the body alert and lighten the mood.

Facilitators have been known to change the whole room setup, using the time when participants are in teams. When people return, they find themselves in a different room, looking at a different set of faces.

If you can use more than one room, or your space is large enough, hold different activities in separate spaces to get people moving around and mixing with others. When participants work with as many people as possible, creative thinking is encouraged.

3. Use humor
It's helpful to remember that laughter is good for the soul and keeps us healthy. Groups that can laugh at themselves have a healthy perspective. The best humor wells up in the facilitator and the group out of the process itself. Often, laughter occurs in the clustering step of the workshop, when the facilitator is striving to get everyone to understand a card. It can help to actually play a little dumb to get the humor to happen to create detachment as the group clarifies the ideas. Use humor to create enough detachment in the group to get the job done.

The injection of humor has been known to backfire, so make sure you know the group and the topic well enough to use humor appropriately. Cynical, belittling and misplaced humor is out of place. Be sensitive to the mood of the group — sometimes humor is needed and at other times an intense discussion is honored by a more serious tone.

4. Be as visual as possible
People can hold visual images much more easily than they can the verbal details of a complex session. Visual images access different parts of the brain and keep the mind active. Whenever possible, use graphs, pictures, tables, and diagrams. A clear display of results helps people integrate new ideas and decisions to take action. Throughout the session, use graphics to display the agenda, the schedule, the process, ground rules, and values. If your handwriting is not easily readable, ask someone else to do the writing. You can give each team differently colored cards to distinguish their work later, or use coloured cards simply for visual appeal. You can even ask participants to draw their answers on cards in addition to writing three to five word titles.

5. Celebrate the group's work

We all thrive on acknowledgment. Affirming people's contributions is a sure way to encourage involvement. Use every opportunity possible to affirm positive participation. Receive and acknowledge individual ideas as they are given. When a small group makes a report, it is quite appropriate to encourage applause. Find appropriate ways for groups to celebrate achievements. At the end of a session, encourage the group to reflect on its progress and celebrate its work.

6. Make each event special

People tend to invest their time and energy in situations that they believe are worthwhile. Try to make each event worthy of the participants' efforts. Inauthenticity is transparent, so create drama and excitement with honesty. Trying to whoop it up in a contradictions analysis (which can be quite painful) may not go over very well. But, in general, much life can come out of an event when much life is put into it. Build anticipation for the event from the first invitation. Special snacks or meals are ways of caring for people; some groups use prizes and games effectively, though sometimes these are inappropriate to the task. Words of encouragement from symbolic leaders can be helpful, especially one who is genuinely concerned or involved.

Some facilitators who have a charismatic or dramatic bent have no trouble in creating eventfulness. But for those of us who distrust charisma or who are not good at drama, these six tactics offer more structural ways to help a group stay involved and engaged throughout the facilitated process.

MANAGING THE GROUP: USING SHORT COURSES

A facilitator needs short, contextual statements to explain the workshop process and deal with misunderstandings as they arise. These mini-interventions in the course of the consensus workshop keep the group on track. They give the group permission to engage in the struggle of the workshop and share pointers on method as needed.

Short courses have been called lecturettes. But that word has unfortunate overtones of the lecture hall and tedious talks. Short courses are really pearls of wisdom, dropped into the group at appropriate moments.

What is a short course?

A short course is a one- or two-sentence statement from the leader that releases or coaches the participants. For example: "Creativity is not something that a only few people have and others don't. You'd be surprised to know how much creativity there is in the people in this group."

Sometimes the short course just says the way it is. For example, "This is the only opportunity we have to deal with this issue. If we don't deal with it now, we'll end up doing what we've always done."

Sometimes a short course consists of words that encourage participation. "There are no wrong answers to a workshop question, so trust your own creativity." Avoid content-related pearls of your own wisdom. Deal with content through questions.

Principles for their use

A few principles for the use of short courses:
- Short courses are not lectures. The best short courses are only one sentence long. For example, "Everyone in this group has wisdom." If your pearl goes on for five minutes, you are lecturing. You are abusing the group by taking time from their participation.
- Short courses are addressed to the whole group, since their intent is to keep the group on track.
- Short courses are not to be used moralistically to beat participants over the head. They need to be used with a very light touch.

Some short courses talk about the way life is: "Life is always full of possibility, no matter what the difficulty." Some are about participation: "Everyone has a piece of the puzzle. The whole picture is attained through hearing and understanding all the perspectives." Some are about group dynamics: "This is the right group of people to wrestle with this issue at this time." Some are related to the use of the method: "Everyone will have an opportunity to hear and be heard."

The following collection of facilitation short courses have proved helpful in various workshop situations and are grouped by type.

Types of short courses

Short courses that say the way it is

1. You have nothing to prove.
2. Life is always full of possibility, no matter what the difficulty.
3. We continue to grow by understanding different viewpoints and insights into today's problems.
4. When you experience yourself angry at an answer, you may need to ask yourself which of your images of life was just questioned.
5. Letting go of your preconceptions of the way life is liberates you to authentically open yourself to the ideas of others.
6. We live out of images that may be true or not — some of them are illusions — we believe they are real, but they are not based on reality.
7. Sometimes some new information we receive pierces our illusions and calls our own understanding into question.
8. Your decision to accept life as good allows you to take any situations that arise and learn from them. That's the kind of acceptance that allows change.

Affirmation Short Courses

1. Life as it is is good — the past is approved, the future is open.
2. This is the right group of people to wrestle with the issue at this time.
3. What happens is what needs to happen; it couldn't have been any other way.
4. This group is at exactly the right place, struggling with the right issues.
5. The group has all the answers and is capable of wrestling with the questions and issues that are facing them.

Method short courses

1. You do not have to agree with any piece of data. You do need to understand it or try to understand it so that you can authentically dialogue with it
2. The whole picture is attained through hearing and understanding all the perspectives.
3. There will be conflicts. Many are surface conflicts from not understanding each other's perspectives and experiences.
4. Use your public voice so that everyone can hear and participate.

The deft application of time and space principles, and the use of eventfulness and short courses can give definition, life, and permission to keep moving as your consensus workshop proceeds.

Part 4

Consensus Workshop Applications

*Chapter 14. Using the Consensus Workshop Method
  with Various Group Sizes*
Chapter 15. Using Consensus Workshops in a Series

The two chapters in this section fill out the consensus workshop uses mentioned in Chapter 1. Someone struggling to master the workshop steps is very happy to pull off one workshop successfully. But as expertise and confidence increase, the facilitator will encounter opportunities for working with much larger groups, and groups in different locations.

Situations will then arise in which one workshop is not enough. The product of one workshop calls for a second and third. The facilitator discovers the need to lead a whole series of workshops.

In this section, you will encounter two new terms: plenary and meta-workshop. When workshops are done in many small teams who then re-gather to share their ideas, this gathering of all the teams is often called a plenary session, or simply, plenary. When the names of the clusters from several workshops become, in turn, the data for a plenary workshop, that latter workshop is sometimes referred to as a meta-workshop, and the collection of all the small-team cluster names as a meta-brainstorm.

14

Using the Consensus Workshop Method with Various Group Sizes

Get them to sit down in groups of about fifty.
The Gospel of Luke

IN THIS CHAPTER we want to show the use of the consensus workshop in groups of different sizes. We will consider groups of the following dimensions:

A. Workshop for an individual
B. Workshop for a small group of two to four
C. Workshop for a group of 5 to 40
D. Workshop for a group of 40 to 100
E. Workshop for a group over 100

Let's start with the smallest group possible — the individual.

A. Workshop for an individual

If you have a particular issue to tackle, you can spend days letting it rattle around in your mind, so you get more anxious by the day. Or you can sit down with a sheet of paper and a pen and do a workshop with yourself. Write down the basic question you are focused on, and brainstorm 15 to 40 ideas for dealing with it. Don't worry about whether you have written something similar earlier in the list — just keep writing. You can either write a list, or put your ideas on sticky notes — one idea per sticky note. Once you have your list, review the ideas you have written down. Begin the clustering and naming as you would in any workshop.

Hints

- Set yourself a target number of ideas, and don't stop until you get there.
- Make sure you cluster ideas by the focus question, and not by cause and effect, or sequentially.
- Ensure that the name you give a cluster is a real answer to the focus question.
- Wring new insight from the data — don't be satisfied with some tired, feeble "same-old" solution. For example, suppose an extraordinary business opportunity is put right under your nose, but you have to be able to put up $50,000 in three month's time. You are dead set on grasping the opportunity.

Focus question

Your focus question is, "What can I do to raise $50,000 in three months?"

Brainstorm

Set yourself to brainstorm 15 ideas. For example brainstorm an unprioritized list like:

1. Hold a family council
2. Get a $10,000 line of credit from one bank
3. Get the same from your second bank
4. Enlist relatives as partners in the task
5. Sell the new business idea to the whole family
6. Second job (at home)
7. Series of garage sales
8. Pawn valuables
9. Commit to three months of austere living
10. Ask John and Joey to deliver papers
11. Get each member of the family to bring in money
12. Sell your TV and VCR and DVD player
13. Sell the SUV
14. Ask boss for a Christmas bonus
15. Cut back key elements of budget by 10 per cent for 3 months
16. Do this workshop with the whole family
17. Target each idea with an amount of money
18. Create a symbol that holds us all to the task

Clustering

You cluster the ideas by using a different symbol for each:

O Hold a family council

X Get a $10,000 line of credit from one bank

X Get the same from your second bank

+ Enlist relatives as partners in the task

O Sell the new business idea to the whole family

Δ Second job (at home)

* Series of garage sales

* Pawn valuables

Three months of austere living

Δ Ask John and Joey to deliver papers

O Get each member of the family to bring in money

* Sell your TV and VCR and DVD player

* Sell the SUV

+ Ask boss for a Christmas bonus

Cut back key elements of budget by 10 per cent for 3 months

O Do this workshop with the whole family

% Target each idea with an amount of money

% Create a symbol that holds us all to the task

Naming

You name each cluster:

O Involve family members

X Secure lines of credit

Δ Expand family jobs

+ Arrange a bonus

* Sell or pawn possessions

Save money by austere living

% Create sustaining symbols

Resolve

You then quickly reflect on the results. You name the next steps, the first of which is to have a family meeting. In this meeting, you will lay out your plan together with your vision for the new business opportunity, and ask for your family's input and cooperation. At this point, you decide you are not going to squeeze the kids. You then put your plan on the door of the fridge, and call the two banks for appointments.

This workshop creates motivation. Instead of moping around, telling yourself how impossible it is to raise money these days, you now have a plan, momentum and a positive story of "This can be done! It is possible!"

B. Workshop for a Small Group of Two to Four

If there are between two and four of you at work, at home or in an informal setting, just talking round a kitchen table can do the job. Each person brainstorms 8 to 12 ideas on sticky notes or cards (one idea per sticky note), so that you will have more than 25 ideas to work with. Each person lays out their five most different or clearest ideas. Find pairs and proceed as you would in a regular consensus workshop. It is easy for people to point to ideas and help move them around; even people who rarely speak in large groups can participate actively.

Hints
The process is the same as in the standard workshop, and the informality gives it a more energetic feel.
- Make sure the focus question and the clustering principle is clear.
- A small group still requires one person to be the facilitator to ask the key questions and keep the process moving.
- Don't let the informality detract from the push for clarity and new insights.

Conversational use
You can even do the consensus workshop process informally in a conversation with someone, as simple questions or a planning exercise. For example:
> I was waiting with my bike at Old Mill Station in Toronto for the train. A young lad was looking rather disconsolate a few steps away. I said, "What's the matter?"
> He said, "My bike has been stolen."
> After commiserating with him, I said, "What are you going to do about it?"
> He said, "Well, I guess I'll have to get a new one, but I have no money. A new one would cost $200."
> I said, "How could you put together $200 to get a new bike?" (focus question). With no great conviction, he named a couple of ways, so I pushed, "What else could you do?" The answers started to tumble out (brainstorm). "So tell me now," I said, "Which of all those ways would you try first? "
> He said, "Paper run, rich uncle, other relatives, mowing lawns, emptying the piggy bank."

I said, "Now are you really serious about this? Do you think you can do it?"

He said, "Yes, I think I can."

"What will you write on your mirror at home to remind you of your decision?"

He thought. Then he said, "New bike by Easter or bust."

C. WORKSHOP FOR A GROUP OF 5 TO 40

You can use the consensus workshop method as described in earlier chapters.

D. WORKSHOP FOR A GROUP OF 40 TO 100

Although coming to consensus with 40 to 100 people in the same room may seem overwhelming, a few adaptations to the card method make it fairly easy.

Here are some hints for working with a large group in one space at the same time:
- Train team facilitators beforehand.
- Make sure each team is answering the same question using the same procedure.
- In the teams, do flip chart workshops or very quick card workshops.
- The titles at the end of the team workshop become the ideas that are placed on cards that go forward to the plenary.

Basically, you need to break such large groups into several small discussion groups for input. The small groups collect input and then report back to pool their insights in a plenary of the whole group.

To do this, you need a team of facilitators for small groups who have to be trained and prepared beforehand. When breaking up into small discussion groups, you need to ensure that each group leader is answering the same question and using the same procedure. The small discussion groups can do flip chart workshops or very quick card workshops. Ensure that people understand that the titles at the end of the team workshop become the ideas that are placed on cards that go forward to the plenary session.
- For the plenary session, make the cards large enough and ask people to write large enough so that the cards can be read by everyone. One idea is to use 8.5 x 11" sheets of card stock.
- If seating is around tables, ask people to move their chairs as close to the front wall as possible so that everyone can see and participate.

When the plenary is finished, the teams may take their decisions back and do further work on implementation, and then share it with the whole group if needed.

Team facilitators

In a large group, each person still has the need to see the range of their ideas on cards and to be confident that they have been heard. At the same time, more than 60 diverse ideas on the wall make for confusion. That large number of cards is not needed for a wise result. How do you balance the need for broad participation and limit the amount of data respectfully at the same time?

The secret is in having teams of 8-15 participants, rather than three to five in the small team brainstorm stage. Divide the total number of cards you want by the number of small teams to decide approximately how many cards each small team should produce. You may want to have more than 60 cards in all with a very large group, but there will be significant overlap of ideas if you get much past 60. With 90 people, for example, you may decide on six teams of 15 people, and ask each team to come back with 10 to 12 cards. The total number of cards will be around 75.

The interactions in a team of 15, however, may still overwhelm a shy or very quiet person, unless the team leader facilitates their participation. Therefore, team leaders for each team need to be trained ahead of time, so that they support the principles of listening for wisdom and inclusiveness that make the larger process work. This supports the whole workshop. In one workshop, a team leader, rather than getting out all the ideas from his team wrote only a few on the cards, ignoring the rest. The whole team was angry when they came to the plenary session, and the lead facilitator had to work hard to make them feel heard.

So, after giving the team their context and inviting everyone to write their own responses to the focus question, the lead facilitator breaks the group into small teams, each with a facilitator.

Procedures for small group brainstorming

(See Chapter 6.)

The purpose of the team work is to get everyone's ideas into the workshop, to make sure everyone is heard and affirmed, and to record diverse input on cards so it can become part of the group's consensus in the plenary session. The steps for a team leader to do this are as follows:

1. Restate the focus question, writing it on a flip chart page for clarity. Tell the group, "In this small group we are going to gather our ideas and put them on cards so that they can be used in the plenary session. There are no wrong answers. We want your real answers to this question. We will list one from each person, then add anything critical that has been left out. We want to end up with about "x" number of different ideas (as assigned by the lead facilitator). As people give their ideas, if you don't understand, ask for clarity or an example. You don't have to agree. You just have to understand."

2. Go around the circle, and have each person list their most important item (in three to four words). Write it on the flip chart in their words.

3. Ask for any critical ideas that didn't get said in the first round.

4. Group similar ideas (to eliminate overlap) to reduce to about "y" number of items. Preserve diversity by putting diverse ideas on separate cards. Keep items as specific as possible, with one idea on each card.

5. Have a couple of people rewrite each idea on the large card — very large and in big, bold print. Try to express each idea in three to four words on the card.

6. Bring the group back to the plenary session. Sit together, spread out your cards so the group can see, and be prepared to send up cards in rounds.

Clustering the data

The plenary clustering is done, as usual, by the lead facilitator.

Naming the clusters

It may also be useful for the same teams to re-gather to do the naming process. Naming in a large group may only get the wisdom of the most assertive people in the room. Try assigning a cluster to each team, and have the facilitator follow the procedures below for the best thinking in a short period of time:

1. Read the cards in your assigned column out loud, or have someone in the group read them out loud.

2. Ask, "What words or phrases struck you as key words in these cards?"

3. "What is this cluster of cards about? What insight does the data here point to?" Explore the underlying theme behind this cluster, in order to answer the focus question.

4. Ask: "What name shall we give to this cluster? Give examples of the kind of name you want to use in this workshop." You may write suggestions from the group on a flip chart page until the group begins to settle on a name that best holds the insights of the column.

The lead facilitator should choose an approach to naming so that all the names are consistent. Some examples:

- Vision — a noun and a juicy descriptive adjective, such as Healthy Environment.
- Obstacles — a three- or four-word phrase that describes a situation that exists, that we are all a part of (beyond blame), that blocks our vision. Usually expressed in the form of: block, how it blocks, what it blocks. For example: Us/Them Mindset Divides Teamwork; or Unpredictable Economy Undermines Long-term Planning.
- Strategic directions — an action with an "–ing" ending and an object of the action. For example: Simplifying Office Procedures; or Starting New Businesses.

5. Bring the title card up and put it on the wall above the column of data.

Resolve

The resolve step is done, as usual, by the lead facilitator as part of the plenary.

E. Workshop for a Group over 100

What if you have to deal, not with five participants or twenty, but hundreds? What then? Well, it's the same thing as before — the hundreds have to be broken up into manageable teams, usually of no more than 20. The procedures are much the same, whether the teams work in separate breakout rooms in the same facility at the same time, or even spread across different times and places. The method works well in a large organization or in companies as well as in the neighborhoods of a city or in different communities in a region.

Naturally, in such large-group work, it's important that each team does exactly the same process. But in designing a large input process, several additional things should be kept in mind:

- Schedule and support team workshops to ensure that you get the broadest participation possible. This may indicate a string of sessions in different locations or at different times.
- The various sessions may be flip chart or card workshops, depending on numbers of people or the time available.
- The column titles from these team workshops become cards in the plenary workshop.
- A representative from each team brings team information to a plenary in which all the teams bring their data together.

- The plenary is a straight-forward workshop. You start with the brainstorm already completed (the titles from the team workshops). Then you sort the brainstorm cards from the team workshops to clarify the major elements in the larger cluster.
- Document the team work. When all the data is documented, you may see new insights not seen in the title cards brought to the plenary meeting.
- Keep all the data that was generated in the team workshops.
- Label cards to indicate the source group. If there are questions about any ideas, the labeling allows rapid checking back to the original source group and original data.

Where the work is being done by teams meeting at different times, it is a good idea to document each team's results on the spot, and bundle the cards tightly to ensure they stay together. Color coding of title cards and data can be a real help as well.

When the plenary is finished, small groups may be organized to take parts of the workshop to the next step on behalf of the large group. The consensus built by this process can be profound in empowering a common direction for a large number of stakeholders.

A large school district, recently merged from several smaller districts, used the team and plenary process to build a consensus of parents, staff, administrators, board, and students to provide a foundation for their future direction. Team workshops were held in seven "families" of schools, and the results brought together in a plenary of 60 people in a hockey arena in the centre of the district. All of the diversity of the new district was held in their plan, and the focus was clear. All the participants went away to implement their plans with a renewed sense of purpose and community.

15

Using the Consensus Workshop Method in a Series

ToP™ methods are highly effective in a variety of situations. They can be used as stand-alone tools, or as part of a series or set. The most dramatic demonstration of their power, however, is when they are woven together into a seminar or program that enables an organization to accomplish major planning tasks.
Laura Spencer

A SEQUENCE OF consensus workshops is needed when one question needs to be answered before the next one can be asked. If you try to cram them both into one workshop, you will probably end up with fuzzy answers to both questions.

When you have the questions, place them in sequence by asking which question needs to be answered first, and which second, so that the answers to the first allow the next question to be answered.

For instance, if you are thinking of putting together a project team, you may need an answer to the question, "What do we have to do to get the best team for this project?" But there is a prior question: "What skills do we need?" You can begin with a workshop on the skills needed, then brainstorm candidates and compare their skills with the skills needed. Then you are ready to deal with the question, "What do we have to do to get them?"

MODEL-BUILDING CONSENSUS WORKSHOP SERIES

A series of workshops is appropriate in situations in which the first workshop paints the broad overview and the following ones develop each of the sub-topics in more depth.

This series begins with the workshop that is the most comprehensive of the set. It starts with a general or visionary focus question like: "What will it take to launch a magazine on global development?" The titles of the column headings in this workshop become the focus questions for another series of workshops. So, if column titles in the first workshop are:
1. A funding plan
2. Themes for the first four issues
3. Assured source of advertising
4. A marketing plan
5. A skilled staff

These may become the topics of workshops at a later date. The focus questions then become:
1. What will it take to ensure adequate funding?
2. What will make our magazine attractive to readers?
3. What do we need to do to win some advertisers?
4. What are the elements of our marketing plan?
5. How do we hire the staff we need?

After all the workshops are completed, the results form a comprehensive model for launching a new magazine.

ToP™ PLANNING SERIES

ToP™ planning is a planning process that has been used in corporations, organizations and communities in more than 50 nations round the world. The ToP™ planning process was originally developed in the early 1970s, and it has been used with corporations, local communities, government agencies, and organizations of all types across the world. For a fuller treatment, see Laura Spencer's *Winning Through Participation* and ICA Canada's *Facilitated Planning Manual*.

This consensus-based planning approach is launched with the formation of a common vision for the organization's future, and ends with the creation of an implementation timeline with assignments, deadlines and scheduled review sessions. It results in a comprehensive and long-ranging plan. Implementation begins the day the planning process is finished.

The consensus-based planning rests on certain assumptions:
- As with most ICA methods, it is highly participatory. It presupposes that everyone knows something that the group needs; that everyone has a piece of the puzzle.
- It does not start from scratch. The group or organization understands its own operational values and will already have clearly stated its mission.
- It assumes that those people who have to implement the plan are participating in the planning. When people create their own plans, they are more likely to implement them. Motivation then comes from within.
- In a corporation, the management will be involved in, or at least aware of the planning, so that it does not feel threatened by the impression of losing control of what is going on.

This consensus-based planning process uses three separate and different workshops, plus a workbook, in the following order:
1. Vision workshop
2. Contradictions workshop
3. Strategic directions workshop
4. Action planning session

The four sessions together generally take two days, but they can be done in one day if necessary. Those familiar with Laura Spencer's *Winning Through Participation* may be thinking, "Wait a minute. What happened to the fifth step?" Laura's step #4 is "Designing the Strategic Actions" and her step #5 is "Drawing up the implementation timeline." However in recent years, many ToP™ facilitators have used only four steps, having found an elegant way to combine the last two of her steps into one — Action Planning. (Figure 25)

In the vision workshop, the participants look at their dreams for the future and draw their ideas into a unified focus to begin the planning. The focus question is either: "What do we want to see going on in our organization in five years?" or "What do we want to see in place in three to five years?" Participants brainstorm their ideas and work in small teams, writing each idea on a card. The cards are clustered according to their intent. Small teams work with each cluster of ideas to determine the common intent of the whole cluster. The result is an image of the community's vision for the future.

Figure 25

In the contradictions (or obstacles) workshop, the participants brainstorm all the obstacles blocking them from moving toward their vision, then cluster and name them to discern the underlying obstacles — the root issues — that both prevent the vision and provide a doorway to achieving them. The core focus question is: "What is blocking us from the realization of our vision?"

The participants then create Strategies to deal with the obstacles and move them toward their vision. They brainstorm answers to the question: "What do we do to deal with the obstacles and release our vision?" They then cluster these actions to reveal new strategies and then cluster the strategies in turn to reveal strategically aligned directions. Finally the group creates short-term action plans to begin to carry out the strategies. Small groups work through a step-by-step process to plan short-term accomplishments and timeline-specific actions to make them happen.

The journey that a participant takes in this kind of planning is from uncertainty to a point of resolve. It could be an individual planning to deal with an issue, or a family plotting a five-year life direction. It could be a team plan, or the community's plan, or the strategic direction of a company or department.

Building Consensus

WORKSHOPS ARE OFTEN used in forming consensus. Therefore it is desirable to get a clear understanding of what consensus is. Otherwise, participants may have different ideas of this elusive goal, and some may be hoping for something utterly impossible.

These points have been found useful in explaining consensus to groups.

1. Consensus is moving forward together

A consensus articulates the common will of the group. Consensus is a common understanding, which enables a group to move forward together. Consensus is reached when all participants are willing to move forward together even if not everyone agrees on all of the details.

2. Consensus is not...

Consensus does not mean total agreement. It does not mean a vote in which some win and some lose, nor does it mean settling for the lowest common denominator or a meaningless abstraction. It does not mean selling a group on an idea, decision or course of action.

3. Consensus is...

The consensus process is thinking things through to the point where the group is able to make appropriate decisions and plans. Consensus is a process of developing commitment, not a way of persuading a group to buy into some preformed concept. The process may involve persuasion, but, most of all, it involves developing a quality dialogue towards the formation of a common mind.

Developing an environment conducive to consensus formation

There are several factors which contribute to the formation of an environment within which consensus can be formed:

1. The participants must have a will to form consensus. It is difficult to arrive at a consensus in situations where an individual or sub-group is determined to impose its will on everyone else.
2. There needs to be a substantial reason or purpose for the formation of consensus. This often takes the form of a clearly delineated focus question, which the group seeks to answer together.
3. All the relevant parties must be included in the dialogue.
4. All ideas must be respected.
5. Forming consensus requires a suspension of assumptions and judgment in order to allow the "new" to emerge.

EXAMPLES OF FOCUS QUESTIONS

The examples of focus questions in the following table show the rational aim for each workshop, the principle for grouping, and the suggested form of the names for the columns.

APPENDIX 2   EXAMPLES OF FOCUS QUESTIONS

Rational Aim	Sample Focus Question	Cluster by:	Suggested Form Name of Columns
Practical vision	What do we want to see in place in this organization in 3-5 years?	Similar characteristics	Juicy adjective, adjective, noun, e.g., state-of-the-art communications department
Outline of a report	What are all the pieces of information to include in this report?	Similar kinds of info — chapters	Adjective noun, e.g., historical influence
Comprehensive definition of scope of negotiation	What are all the possible topics we want to cover in this negotiation? (What is the scope of this negotiation?)	Similar topics	Adjective noun, e.g., legal issues
Action plans to do project	What are all the things we need to do to accomplish this project?	Actions that can be done together	Gerund noun, e.g., cleaning grounds
List of shared values to consider when buying a house	What values do we want to hold in buying a new house?	Similar values	Phrase, e.g., easy access to outdoors
List of shared elements to include in holiday plans	What are elements of a successful holiday?	Similar components	Adjective noun, e.g., quiet time
Strategies	What can we do to deal with these obstacles?	Actions that can be done together	Gerund noun, e.g., starting new business
Description of qualities to work toward as a team	What are the qualities of a high performance work team?	Similar qualities	Juicy adjective or metaphor, e.g., respectful
Basic attributes for a "dohickey"	What attributes are needed for this "dohickey" to work well?	Similar attributes	Juicy adjective noun, e.g., slick wheels
Underlying obstacles that block us	What blocks are we running into?	Underlying root issues	Descriptive phrase, e.g., undeveloped personal capacity
Consensus on solution to problem	What are elements of a solution to this problem?	Similar components of a solution	Adjective noun, e.g., focused training
Framework	What are all the things we need to include in our overall framework?	Similar elements of framework	Adjective noun, e.g., informal network
Improvement plan	What are all the things we could do to improve our team performance?	Similar actions	Verb object, e.g., hold regular meetings
Task forces action plan for successful conference	What do we have to do to make our conference really successful?	Actions that can be done by same group	Task force name, e.g., registrations
Values for dealing with topic	What are all the things we have to consider in approaching this topic?	Similar considerations	Adjective noun, e.g., personal feelings
Definition of research topic	What are all the questions we have regarding this topic?	Similar underlying question	Simple question, e.g., What are the historical events that had an impact?
Shared vision of a healthy community	If you were looking for a healthy community to move to in the next year, what factors or identifying characteristics would you consider?	Similar characteristics	Juicy adjective noun, e.g., lively commercial activity

ICA: Its Mission and Locations

THE INSTITUTE OF Cultural Affairs is a not-for-profit organization concerned with equipping people to make a difference in communities and organizations. Its work at present includes facilitation, consulting, training, research and publications.

For 45 years, ICA has been a presence in adult and child education, in community reformulation projects around the world, in organizational development, and in researching and testing the intellectual tools and social methods needed by people participating in social change.

In 2002, ICA is a presence in 28 countries spread across six continents. The ICA office in each nation is autonomous. ICA International, headquartered in Brussels, acts as a clearinghouse for information and a coordination centre for the national ICAs.

At present, teaching courses in facilitation methods is a focus for several ICA offices. The Group Facilitation course, which features the conversation method and the workshop method, is taught on a regular basis in the ICA locations listed below. From these sources, you can obtain information about this course and the dates on which it will be held, and on other ICA offerings.

ICA International

Rue Amedee Lynen #8
B-1210 Brussels
Belgium
icai@linkline.be
Tel.: (32 2) 219 0087
Fax: (32 2) 219 0406
Web site: www.icaworld.org/
E-mail: icai@linkline.be

Canada

ICA Associates
579 Kingston Rd
Toronto, Ontario, Canada
M4E 1R3
Tel.: (1 416) 691-2316
Fax: (1 416) 691-2491
E-mail: ica@icacan.ca
Web site: www.icacan.ca

United States

Web site: www.ica-usa.org

ICA Eastern States: Member Services
248 Second Street
Troy, NY 12180, USA
Tel.: (1 518) 273 6797
E-mail: icatroy@igc.apc.org

ICA Heartland/Chicago
4750 N. Sheridan Road
Chicago, IL 60640, USA
Tel.: (1 773) 769 6363
Fax: (1 773) 769 1144
E-mail: icachicago@igc.apc.org

ICA Western States/Phoenix
4220 North 25th Street
Phoenix, AZ 85016 USA
Tel.: (1 602) 955 4811
FAX:(1 602) 954 0563
E-mail: icaphoenix@igc.apc.org

BIBLIOGRAPHY

Books

Bergdall, Terry D. *Methods for Active Participation: Experiences in Rural Development from Central and East Africa*. Oxford University Press, Nairobi, 1993.

Doyle, Michael and David Straus. *How to Make Meetings Work: The New Interaction Method*. Berkeley Books, New York, 1976.

Jenkins, John. *International Facilitator's Companion Imaginal Training*. Groningen, Netherlands, 1996.

Kaner, Sam, et al. *Facilitator's Guide to Participatory Decision-Making*. New Society Publishers, Gabriola Island, British Columbia, 1996.

General Henry Robert. *Rules of Order: The Standard Guide to Parliamentary Procedure*. Bantam Books, Toronto, 1982.

Schein, Edgar H. *Process Consultation Volumes I and II: Lessons for Managers and Consultants*. Addison-Wesley Publishing Company, Reading, Massachusetts, 1997.

Schwarz , Roger M. *The Skilled Facilitator: Practical Wisdom for Developing Effective Groups*. Jossey-Bass, San Francisco, 1994.

Spencer, Laura. *Winning Through Participation: The Technology of Participation*. Kendall-Hunt Publishing Company, Dubuque, Iowa, 1989.

Stanfield, R. Brian. *The Art of Focused Conversation*. New Society Publishers, Gabriola Island, British Columbia, 1997.

Weaver, Richard and John Farrell. *Managers As Facilitators*. Berrett-Koehler Publishers, Inc., San Francisco, 1997.

Williams, R. Bruce. *More Than 50 Ways to Build Team Consensus*. IRI Skylight Training and Publishing, Arlington Heights, Illinois, 1993.

Wright, Susan and David Morley. *Learning Works: Searching for Organizational Futures*. Faculty of Environmental Studies, York University, Toronto, 1989.

List Serves

Ruete, Edward S. The Proceedings of the International Association of Facilitators: "Group Facilitation" List Serve, 24 March 1997.

Periodicals

Jenkins, Jon. "Disciplines of the Facilitator." *Edges.* August 2000, pp 2-4.

Stanfield, Brian. "Mapping Organizations." *Edges*, August 1997. pp 2-5.

Stanfield, Brian. "The Magic of the Facilitator." *Edges.* September 1994, pp 3-7.

Nelson, Wayne. "Facilitator Style." *Edges.* April 1997, p 6.

Nelson, Wayne. "Creating Eventfulness." *Edges.* September 1996, p 5.

Presentations

Holmes, Duncan. "Public Meetings That Build Community," [presentation, unpublished manuscript] The Nova Scotia Planners' Conference, Halifax, 1998.

Training Manuals

ICA Associates Inc. *Group Facilitation* (revised). Toronto, 2001.

ICA Associates Inc. *Facilitated Planning* (revised). Toronto, 2001 .

ICA Associates Inc. *Meetings That Work*. Toronto, 2000.

ICA Associates Inc. *Participation Paradigm* (revised). Toronto, 2001.

ICA Associates Inc. *Power of Image Change in Transformation*. Toronto, 2001.

Video

Staples, Bill. *Technology of Participation*. [training video] ICA Canada, 1993.

INDEX

THE CANADIAN INSTITUTE OF CULTURAL AFFAIRS

The Canadian Institute of Cultural Affairs, a non-profit organization, builds people's capacity for shared social responsibility by researching, publishing, teaching, and demonstrating participatory approaches to learning, leadership, planning, and action. In January 2001, ICA Canada celebrated its 25th anniversary as a registered Canadian charitable organization.

ICA is a global non-profit social change organization that has existed for 45 years. Today it operates in over 32 countries on six continents.

The current scope of ICA's activities in Canada includes sharing experience and knowledge in social capacity building methods through:
- publishing newsletters, periodicals, manuals, and books
- research on social innovations, needs, trends, and models
- education and learning through conferences, forums, and study groups
- projects in individual and community development and leadership.

In October 1999, ICA Associates Inc. was created as a for-profit organization to distribute ICA Canada's knowledge through training, facilitation, and consultation.

Other resources available from The Canadian Institute of Cultural Affairs and ICA Associates Inc. :
> *The Art of Focused Conversation: 100 Ways to Access Group Wisdom in the Workplace.* R. Brian Stanfield (222 pages).
> *The Courage To Lead: Transform Self, Transform Society.* R. Brian Stanfield (260 pages).
> *The Art of Focused Conversation for Schools: Over 100 Ways to Guide Clear Thinking and Promote Learning.* Jo Nelson (268 pages).

How To Contact Us

By mail: The Canadian Institute of Cultural Affairs
579 Kingston Rd
Toronto, ON Canada
M4E 1R3
By telephone: (416) 691 2316
Toll-free (outside of Toronto and in Canada) (1877) 691 1422
By fax: (416) 691 2491
By e-mail: ica@icacan.ca
Web site: www.icacan.ca

Books to Build A New Society

New Society Publishers' mission
is to publish books that contribute in fundamental ways
to building an ecologically sustainable and just society,
and to do so with the least possible impact on the environment,
in a manner that models that vision.

If you have enjoyed *The Workshop Book*,
you may also want to check out our other titles
in the following categories:

Progressive Leadership
Ecological Design & Planning
Environment & Justice
New Forestry
Accountable Economics
Conscientious Commerce
Resistance & Community
Educational & Parenting Resources

For a full list of NSP's titles,
please call 1-800-567-6772,
or check out our website at:
www.newsociety.com

NEW SOCIETY PUBLISHERS